9 95
-5

Six Centuries of Verse

Six Centuries of Verse

Selected and introduced by
ANTHONY THWAITE

Thames Methuen

821.009
SIX
1985

First published in the U.S.A. 1985 by
Methuen, Inc., 733 Third Avenue, New York, N.Y. 10017
First published in Great Britain 1984
by Methuen London Ltd
11 New Fetter Lane, London EC4P 4EE
in association with
Thames Television International Ltd
149 Tottenham Court Road, London WIP 9LL
Reprinted 1985
Selection and introductory material
copyright © 1984 Anthony Thwaite
Printed in Great Britain by
Redwood Burn Ltd., Trowbridge

ISBN 0 423 00950 8 hardback
     0 423 00960 5 paperback

British Library cataloguing in publication data:
Six centuries of verse.
  1. English poetry—History and criticism
  I. Thwaite, Anthony
  821'.009   PR502

Eastern   4/24/86.   9.95   8.96-paper

Contents

List of Illustrations

page

Preface

Arnold Bennett, a writer of straightforwardness and bluff common sense if nothing else, once wrote:

> There is a word . . . which rouses terror in the heart of the vast educated majority of the English-speaking race . . . I myself have seen it empty buildings that had been full . . . Even to murmur it is to incur solitude, probably disdain, and possibly starvation, as historical examples show. That word is 'poetry'.

Bennett may have been right. The English in general do seem embarrassed by it – perhaps embarrassed rather than indifferent. And yet English poetry has a longer continuous history of excellence than any other in the world (even the French and the Japanese might be prepared to give way on this), and our poets have been internationally recognised in a way that has only sporadically been true of our painters, sculptors or composers.

If someone in, shall we say, a Manchester pub responds to a stranger's question 'What's your work?' with 'I'm a poet', that person will almost certainly be taken to be a fool, or effeminate, or drunk. It will be supposed that the 'poet' will take a daffodil out of his pocket, or start talking in a high piping voice about 'Beauty'. Daffodils and Beauty are, to be sure, part of poetry; but so are Manchester pubs, anger, every kind of sexuality, the love of God, grief, depression, dreams, jokes, story-telling, things both grave and what one used to call gay, and much else. The English temperament and English poetry – both of them complex mixtures of the same thing – have included them all; and they still do.

This book is an attempt to give a guided tour of English poetry from Chaucer to the present day. It is a tour rather than a literary history or a straightforward anthology, though it has elements of both. The tour is chronological, with each section an amalgam of introduction and comment alongside the poems themselves.

The book was written as a companion to the Thames Television series shown on Channel 4, 'Six Centuries of Verse', presented by Sir John Gielgud; but it is also intended to be self-sufficient, capable of being read with enjoyment by those who did not see the programmes. I have included work by poets I had, regretfully, to exclude from the series because of the constraints of timing (Sidney, Spenser, Herrick, Lovelace, Suckling and others), as well as a rather broader representation of some of the poets already included. To make the book useful as a reference work as well as being a narrative anthology, I have added at the back a section of biographical and bibliographical notes on each poet.

The texts reproduced are inconsistent. With earlier poems, sometimes I have used the original spelling, sometimes a modernised version, and my choice has been dictated by what I feel is appropriate to the work. *The Faerie Queene* and *Paradise Lost* seem to me to benefit from the original spelling; Shakespeare – except perhaps in his sonnets – does not. Chaucer is a special case and, except for the opening of the General Prologue to *The Canterbury Tales* (which is given in both the original and in translation), I have fallen back on Nevill Coghill's version.

For a great deal of work on the illustrations, I am grateful to Julia Brown. I am also grateful to Diana Potter and Richard Mervyn of Thames Television, executive producer and director of the series, who commissioned and encouraged me in the first place, and with whom I worked closely as the programmes were put together. The Thames Television crews and the various actors who took part were a liberal education to me, and I enjoyed their company. Sir John Gielgud, in particular, helped me in the most restrained and friendly fashion, by mildly suggesting now and then that some of the words of commentary I had given him to speak were unspeakable. I hope the result is clarity.

November 1983

1. A portrait of
Chaucer from
Hoccleve's *De Regimine
Principum*, early 15th
century.

ONE

Chaucer
1340-1400

It took more than three centuries after the Norman Conquest of 1066 for
our language to evolve into something which we can immediately
recognise as the direct ancestor of English as we know it today; and we
recognise it most directly in the work of the first great named poet in our
literature, Geoffrey Chaucer. In Chaucer's *Canterbury Tales*, written
probably during the last fifteen or so years of his life, we see a language, a
spirit and a view of humanity which still speak to us: we respond to
Chaucer without the scholarly intermediaries that are almost always
necessary when we come to such contemporary poems as *Gawain and the
Green Knight* or *Piers Plowman*.

2. An early view of
London, a woodcut
from Richard Pynson's
1510 edition of
Cronycle of Englande.

3. (right) Pilgrims leaving
Canterbury.

4. (below) The Gough map of
south-east England shows the
distance Chaucer's pilgrims had
to travel from London:
Canterbury is near the
easternmost tip of Kent.

This is partly because Chaucer used that dialect of the East Midlands and London, influenced by Norman-French, which gradually became modern English, whereas the *Gawain* poet and William Langland (the supposed author of *Piers Plowman*) used the more archaic speech of the West Midlands and, in addition, the old-fashioned alliterative verse which derived ultimately from Old English, or Anglo-Saxon. Chaucer's 'Middle English', as it is called, is closer to us than anything that went before.

So, indeed, are the people about whom Chaucer wrote. *The Canterbury Tales* is a long sequence of verse stories, mostly linked together by introductions and prologues supposed to be spoken by the characters themselves: a knight and his squire, a merchant, a lawyer, a doctor, a cook, a miller and many people connected with the Church – a parson, a prioress, a friar, a pardoner and so on. It is in fact a cross-section of medieval society, very sharp-eyed in its observation, often slyly funny in the way Chaucer describes his characters in the General Prologue to the *Tales* and in the way they seem to present themselves in their own introductions.

All the characters are going on pilgrimage to the shrine of Thomas à Becket at Canterbury; and before they set out to ride together from Southwark in London to Canterbury, they decide to entertain one another with stories. In the General Prologue, Chaucer gives us, in the first forty lines, the time of year, the purpose of the visit, the setting at the start, the number of the pilgrims (about twenty-nine of them), the fact that the poet himself is one of them, and the introduction to the cast list. Here are those opening lines, first in the original, probably written some time in the late 1380s, then in the modern verse translation by Nevill Coghill:

The Prologue

Whán that Apríllė with his shourės soote
The droghte of March hath percėd to the roote,
And bathed every veyne in swich licóur
Of which vertú engendred is the flour;
Whan Zephirus eek with his swetė breeth
Inspirėd hath in every holt and heeth
The tendrė croppės, and the yongė sonne
Hath in the Ram his halfė cours y-ronne,
And smalė fowelės maken melodye,
That slepen al the nyght with open eye, –
So priketh hem Natúre in hir coráges, –
Thanne longen folk to goon on pilgrimages,

And palmeres for to seken straungė strondes,
To fernė halwės, kowthe in sondry londes;
And specially, from every shirės ende
Of Engėlond, to Caunterbury they wende,
The hooly blisful martir for to seke,
That hem hath holpen whan that they were seeke.

Bifil that in that seson on a day,
In Southwerk at the Tabard as I lay,
Redy to wenden on my pilgrymage
To Caunterbury with ful devout corage,
At nyght were come into that hostelrye
Wel nyne-and-twenty in a compaignye,
Of sondry folk, by áventure y-falle
In felaweshipe, and pilgrimes were they alle,
That toward Caunterbury wolden ryde.
The chambres and the stables weren wyde,
And wel we weren esėd attė beste.
And shortly, whan the sonnė was to reste,
So haddė I spoken with hem everychon,
That I was of hir felaweshipe anon,
And madė forward erly for to ryse,
To take oure wey ther, as I yow devyse.
But nathėless, whil I have tyme and space,
Er that I ferther in this talė pace,
Me thynketh it accordaunt to resoun
To tellė yow al the condicioun
Of ech of hem, so as it semėd me,
And whiche they weren and of what degree,
And eek in what array that they were inne;
And at a Knyght than wol I first bigynne.

*   *   *

When the sweet showers of April fall and shoot
Down through the drought of March to pierce the root,
Bathing every vein in liquid power
From which there springs the engendering of the flower,
When also Zephyrus with his sweet breath
Exhales an air in every grove and heath
Upon the tender shoots, and the young sun
His half-course in the sign of the *Ram* has run,
And the small fowl are making melody
That sleep away the night with open eye
(So nature pricks them and their heart engages)

Then people long to go on pilgrimages
And palmers long to seek the stranger strands
Of far-off saints, hallowed in sundry lands,
And specially, from every shire's end
In England, down to Canterbury they wend
To seek the holy blissful martyr, quick
In giving help to them when they were sick.
    It happened in that season that one day
In Southwark, at *The Tabard*, as I lay
Ready to go on pilgrimage and start
For Canterbury, most devout at heart.
At night there came into that hostelry
Some nine and twenty in a company
Of sundry folk happening then to fall
In fellowship, and they were pilgrims all
That towards Canterbury meant to ride.
The rooms and stables of the inn were wide;
They made us easy, all was of the best.
And shortly, when the sun had gone to rest,
By speaking to them all upon the trip
I was admitted to their fellowship
And promised to rise early and take the way
To Canterbury, as you heard me say.
    But none the less, while I have time and space,
Before my story takes a further pace,
It seems a reasonable thing to say
What their condition was, the full array
Of each of them, as it appeared to me,
According to profession and degree,
And what apparel they were riding in;
And at a Knight I therefore will begin.

The Knight, indeed, tells the first of the twenty-four stories – a suitable tale of love and chivalry, in keeping with his personality. Later on Chaucer himself pretends to tell a story but deliberately makes it so boring and amateurish that the Host of the Inn at Southwark, who is travelling with them, stops him abruptly in mid-career:

'By God,' quod he, 'for pleynly, at a word,
Thy drasty rymyng is nat worth a toord!'

('By God,' he said, 'put plainly in a word,
Your dreary rhyming isn't worth a turd!')

Among the characters connected with the Church there is one particularly unpleasant fellow: the Pardoner. Pardoners were minor but powerful Church officers whose job it was – with presumed authority from the Pope – to sell divine forgiveness for money. Naturally enough, they were not popular figures; and when Chaucer in the Prologue comes to describe this particular one, we are left in no doubt about his loathesomeness – though Chaucer, as usual, suggests it ironically, rather than attacking him head-on:

from The Prologue

This Pardoner had hair as yellow as wax
Hanging down smoothly like a hank of flax.
In driblets fell his locks behind his head
Down to his shoulders which they overspread;
Thinly they fell, like rat-tails, one by one.
He wore no hood upon his head, for fun;
The hood inside his wallet had been stowed,
He aimed at riding in the latest mode;
But for a little cap his head was bare
And he had bulging eye-balls, like a hare.
He'd sowed a holy relic on his cap;
His wallet lay before him on his lap,
Brimful of pardons come from Rome all hot.
He had the same small voice a goat has got.
His chin no beard had harboured, nor would harbour,
Smoother than ever chin was left by barber.
I judge he was a gelding, or a mare.
As to his trade, from Berwick down to Ware
There was no pardoner of equal grace,
For in his trunk he had a pillow-case
Which he asserted was Our Lady's veil.
He said he had a gobbet of the sail
Saint Peter had the time when he made bold
To walk the waves, till Jesu Christ took hold.
He had a cross of metal set with stones
And, in a glass, a rubble of pigs' bones.
And with these relics, any time he found
Some poor up-country parson to astound,
On one short day, in money down, he drew
More than the parson in a month or two,
And by his flatteries and prevarication
Made monkeys of the priest and congregation.

But still to do him justice first and last
In church he was a noble ecclesiast.
How well he read a lesson or told a story!
But best of all he sang an Offertory,
For well he knew that when that song was sung
He'd have to preach and tune his honey-tongue
And (well he could) win silver from the crowd.
That's why he sang so merrily and loud.

The tale the Pardoner tells later on is one of the most effective in the whole of *The Canterbury Tales*, about three young gamblers who set out to kill Death and steal his money, but whose greed spells their own ruin. The story is dramatically direct and powerful in its simplicity. Before the story itself begins, the Pardoner – entirely in character – lays his hypocritical bait by giving plenty of ghastly moral examples about drinking, gambling, swearing and greed. His story is meant to compel the audience to repent such evil ways. When he has finished, he tries to sell some of his holy relics and pardons – and is promptly given a rude reply by the Host of the Inn. But the story itself has made its point:

The Pardoner's Tale

It's of three rioters I have to tell
Who long before the morning service bell
Were sitting in a tavern for a drink.
And as they sat, they heard the hand-bell clink
Before a coffin going to the grave;
One of them called the little tavern-knave
And said 'Go and find out at once – look spry! –
Whose corpse is in that coffin passing by;
And see you get the name correctly too.'
'Sir,' said the boy, 'no need, I promise you;
Two hours before you came here I was told.
He was a friend of yours in days of old,
And suddenly, last night, the man was slain,
Upon his bench, face up, dead drunk again.
There came a privy thief, they call him Death,
Who kills us all round here, and in a breath
He speared him through the heart, he never stirred.
And then Death went his way without a word.
He's killed a thousand in the present plague,
And, sir, it doesn't do to be too vague

If you should meet him; you had best be wary.
Be on your guard with such an adversary,
Be primed to meet him everywhere you go,
That's what my mother said. It's all I know.'
    The publican joined in with, 'By St Mary,
What the child says is right; you'd best be wary,
This very year he killed, in a large village
A mile away, man, woman, serf at tillage,
Page in the household, children – all there were.
Yes, I imagine that he lives round there.
It's well to be prepared in these alarms,
He might do you dishonour.' 'Huh, God's arms!'
The rioter said, 'Is he so fierce to meet?
I'll search for him, by Jesus, street by street.
God's blessed bones! I'll register a vow!
Here, chaps! The three of us together now,
Hold up your hands, like me, and we'll be brothers
In this affair, and each defend the others,
And we will kill this traitor Death, I say!
Away with him as he has made away
With all our friends. God's dignity! To-night!'
    They made their bargain, swore with appetite,
These three, to live and die for one another
As brother-born might swear to his born brother.
And up they started in their drunken rage
And made towards this village which the page
And publican had spoken of before.
Many and grisly were the oaths they swore,
Tearing Christ's blessed body to a shred;
'If we can only catch him, Death is dead!'
    When they had gone not fully half a mile,
Just as they were about to cross a stile,
They came upon a very poor old man
Who humbly greeted them and thus began.
'God look to you, my lords, and give you quiet!'
To which the proudest of these men of riot
Gave back the answer, 'What, old fool? Give place!
Why are you all wrapped up except your face?
Why live so long? Isn't it time to die?'
    The old, old fellow looked him in the eye
And said, 'Because I never yet have found,
Though I have walked to India, searching round
Village and city on my pilgrimage,
One who would change his youth to have my age.

And so my age is mine and must be still
Upon me, for such time as God may will.
　'Not even Death, alas, will take my life;
So, like a wretched prisoner at strife
Within himself, I walk alone and wait
About the earth, which is my mother's gate,
Knock-knocking with my staff from night to noon
And crying, "Mother, open to me soon!
Look at me, mother, won't you let me in?
See how I wither, flesh and blood and skin!
Alas! When will these bones be laid to rest?
Mother, I would exchange – for that were best –

5. Part of the Ellesmere manuscript of 'The Pardoner's Tale' with a picture of the Pardoner.

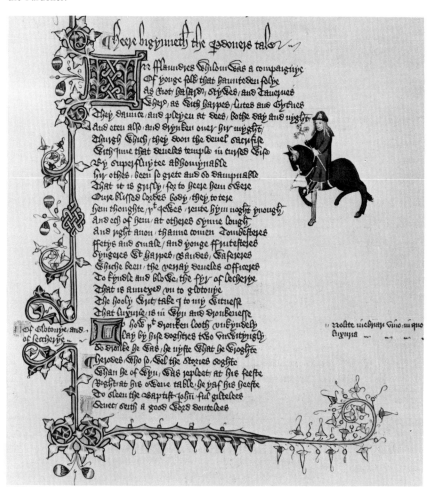

The wardrobe in my chamber, standing there
So long, for yours! Aye, for a shirt of hair
To wrap me in!" She has refused her grace,
Whence comes the pallor of my withered face.
　'But it dishonoured you when you began
To speak so roughly, sir, to an old man,
Unless he had injured you in word or deed.
It says in holy writ, as you may read,
"Thou shalt rise up before the hoary head
And honour it," and therefore be it said
"Do no more harm to an old man than you,
Being now young, would have another do
When you are old" – if you should live till then.
And so may God be with you, gentlemen,
For I must go whither I have to go.'
　'By God,' the gambler said, 'you shan't do so,
You don't get off so easy, by St John!
I heard you mention, just a moment gone,
A certain traitor Death who singles out
And kills the fine young fellows hereabout,
And you're his spy, by God! You wait a bit.
Say where he is or you shall pay for it,
By God and by the Holy Sacrament!
I say you've joined together by consent
To kill us younger folk, you thieving swine!'
　'Well, sirs,' he said, 'if it be your design
To find out Death, turn up this crooked way
Towards that grove, I left him there to-day
Under a tree, and there you'll find him waiting.
He isn't one to hide for all your prating.
You see that oak? He won't be far to find.
And God protect you that redeemed mankind,
Aye, and amend you!' Thus that ancient man.
　At once the three young rioters began
To run, and reached the tree, and there they found
A pile of golden florins on the ground,
New-coined, eight bushels of them as they thought.
No longer was it Death those fellows sought,
For they were all so thrilled to see the sight,
The florins were so beautiful and bright,
That down they sat beside the precious pile.
The wickedest spoke first after a while.
'Brothers,' he said, 'you listen to what I say.
I'm pretty sharp although I joke away.

It's clear that Fortune has bestowed this treasure
To let us live in jollity and pleasure
Light come, light go! We'll spend it as we ought.
God's precious dignity! Who would have thought
This morning was to be our lucky day?
 'If one could get the gold away,
Back to my house, or else to yours, perhaps –
For as you know, the gold is ours, chaps –
We'd all be at the top of fortune, hey?
But certainly it can't be done by day.
People would call us robbers – a strong gang,
So our own property would make us hang.
No, we must bring this treasure back by night
Some prudent way, and keep it out of sight.
And so as a solution I propose
We draw for lots and see the way it goes,
The one who draws the longest, lucky man,
Shall run to town as quickly as he can
To fetch us bread and wine – but keep things dark –
While two remain in hiding here to mark
Our heap of treasure. If there's no delay,
When night comes down we'll carry it away,
All three of us, wherever we have planned.'
 He gathered lots and hid them in his hand
Bidding them draw for where the luck should fall.
It fell upon the youngest of them all,
And off he ran at once towards the town.
 As soon as he had gone the first sat down
And thus began a parley with the other:
'You know that you can trust me as a brother;
Now let me tell you where your profit lies;
You know our friend has gone to get supplies
And here's a lot of gold that is to be
Divided equally amongst us three.
Nevertheless, if I could shape things thus
So that we shared it out – the two of us –
Wouldn't you take it as a friendly turn?'
 'But how?' the other said with some concern.
'Because he knows the gold's with me and you;
What can we tell him? What are we to do?'
 'Is it a bargain,' said the first, 'or no?
For I can tell you in a word or so
What's to be done to bring the thing about.'
'Trust me,' the other said, 'you needn't doubt

My work. I won't betray you, I'll be true.'
  'Well,' said his friend, 'you see that we are two,
And two are twice as powerful as one.
Now look; when he comes back, get up in fun
To have a wrestle; then, as you attack,
I'll up and put my dagger through his back
While you and he are struggling, as in game;
Then draw your dagger too and do the same.
Then all this money will be ours to spend,
Divided equally of course, dear friend.
When we can gratify our lusts and fill
The day with dicing at our own sweet will.'
Thus these two miscreants agreed to slay
The third and youngest, as you heard me say.
  The youngest, as he ran towards the town,
Kept turning over, rolling up and down
Within his heart the beauty of those bright
New florins, saying, 'Lord, to think I might
Have all that treasure to myself alone!
Could there be anyone beneath the throne
Of God so happy as I then should be?'
  And so the Fiend, our common enemy,
Was given power to put it in his thought
That there was always poison to be bought,
And that with poison he could kill his friends.
To men in such a state the Devil sends
Thoughts of this kind, and has a full permission
To lure them on to sorrow and perdition;
For this young man was utterly content
To kill them both and never to repent.
  And on he ran, he had no thought to tarry,
Came to the town, found an apothecary
And said, 'Sell me some poison if you will,
I have a lot of rats I want to kill
And there's a polecat too about my yard
That takes my chickens and it hits me hard;
But I'll get even, as is only right,
With vermin that destroy a man by night.'
  The chemist answered, 'I've a preparation
Which you shall have, and by my soul's salvation
If any living creature eat or drink
A mouthful, ere he has the time to think,
Though he took less than makes a grain of wheat,
You'll see him fall down dying at your feet;

Yes, die he must, and in so short a while
You'd hardly have the time to walk a mile,
The poison is so strong, you understand.'
    This cursed fellow grabbed into his hand
The box of poison and away he ran
Into a neighbouring street, and found a man
Who lent him three large bottles. He withdrew
And deftly poured the poison into two.
He kept the third one clean, as well he might,
For his own drink, meaning to work all night
Stacking the gold and carrying it away.
And when this rioter, this devil's clay,
Had filled his bottles up with wine, all three,
Back to rejoin his comrades sauntered he.
    Why make a sermon of it? Why waste breath?
Exactly in the way they'd planned his death
They fell on him and slew him, two to one.
Then said the first of them when this was done
'Now for a drink. Sit down and let's be merry,
For later on there'll be the corpse to bury.'
And, as it happened, reaching for a sup,
He took a bottle full of poison up
And drank; and his companion, nothing loth,
Drank from it also, and they perished both.
    There is, in Avicenna's long relation
Concerning poison and its operation,
Trust me, no ghastlier section to transcend
What these two wretches suffered at their end.
Thus these two murderers received their due,
So did the treacherous young poisoner too.

When Chaucer died, in 1400, he was already a famous poet. He had spent almost the whole of his working life at the centre of affairs, as a courtier, a diplomat and a civil servant; and in such positions he had been well placed not only to observe a wide range of varied human beings but also to be recognised as a poet. He had a ready-made available audience of sophisticated and sympathetic people, the educated minority of his day. It is partly this that gives Chaucer his ease of tone, which we notice even now, almost six centuries after his death. He was speaking directly and without strain to people who understood and accepted him – the wide cross-section of life represented in the courts of Edward III, Richard II, John of Gaunt and Henry IV.

Apart from the enormous achievement of *The Canterbury Tales*, Chaucer wrote many other long poems, from the mixed dream-vision and satire of his translation from the French, the *Romance of the Rose*, to the complex dramatic narrative of *Troilus and Criseyde*. He found much of his source material in such ancient writers as Ovid and Virgil, and in the Italian writers of his own epoch, such as Boccaccio, Petrarch and Dante. But from them all, and particularly in *The Canterbury Tales*, he made something peculiarly English. He was a sophisticated craftsman who had a strong sense of the everyday, and he could use verse to be descriptive, funny, moralising, narrative, with directness, shrewdness and a novelist's eye for the telling detail. He belongs, by chronology, to the Middle Ages, but he can often seem uncannily 'modern': we can still recognise ourselves in his inventions.

6. A manuscript illustration of Chaucer reading from *Troilus and Criseyde* to the court of Richard II.

TWO

Medieval to Elizabethan
1400 - 1600

In the two centuries following the death of Chaucer in 1400, the Middle Ages merge into that rediscovery of the classical world of Greece and Rome which became known as the Renaissance – a slow and complex process which affected all thought and science, and all the arts. But from the Middle Ages and well into the sixteenth century there survive hundreds of anonymous poems, or poems by writers who, if their identities were ever known, have been lost to us. These are the poems of the ordinary people. Some of them are love-songs, some are ballads or story-telling poems, some are lyrics about spring, or ploughing, or death. Some are the earliest nursery rhymes and lullabies in our language. And very many are carols – not just Christmas carols, but celebrations of all the great feast-days of the Church, often intended to be accompanied by dancing. One of the best known is in fact a Christmas carol, a simple poem of adoration, wonder and praise of the Virgin Mary, composed perhaps late in the fifteenth or early in the sixteenth century:

I sing of a maiden

I sing of a maiden
That is makeles:
King of alle kinges
To here sone she ches.

He cam also stille
Ther his moder was,
As dew in Aprille
That falleth on the grass.

He cam also stille
To his moderes bowr,
As dew in Aprille
That falleth on the flowr.

He cam also stille
Ther his moder lay,
As dew in Aprille
That falleth on the spray.

Moder and maiden
Was never non but she:
Well may swich a lady
Godes moder be.

Some of these early carols are mysterious – or at least mysterious to us. One of these is known as the 'Corpus Christi Carol'. At one level, it seems to be about the Crucifixion, the Holy Grail, the Eucharist; but some historians and scholars have seen in it a hint or reference to Anne Boleyn, one of Henry VIII's disgraced wives, executed for supposed adultery. Whatever the answer to the riddle, the poem is very strange and haunting:

Corpus Christi Carol

Lully, lulley, lully, lulley,
The fawcon hath born my mak away.

He bare him up, he bare him down,
He bare him into an orchard brown.

In that orchard ther was an hall,
That was hangèd with purpill and pall.

And in that hall ther was a bed:
It was hangèd with gold so red.

And in that bed ther lythe a knight,
His woundès bleeding day and night.

By that bedès side ther kneleth a may,
And she wepeth both night and day.

And by that bedès side ther stondeth a ston,
'Corpus Christi' wreten theron.

One of the late medieval poets we do know a good deal about, partly because he was a well-known, even notorious, figure at the courts of Henry VII and the young Henry VIII (to whom he had been tutor before

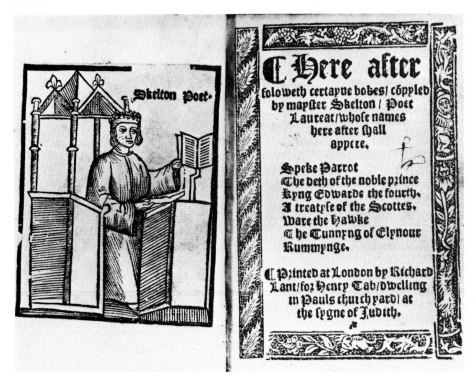

7. A woodcut, c. 1545, of Skelton from
Certayn Bokes coppied by Mayster Skelton Poet Laureat.

Henry came to the throne), is John Skelton. Skelton was born about sixty years after Chaucer's death. He was a court poet for much of his life, was equally at home at Oxford and Cambridge, and was a laureate of both universities, as well as *Orator Regius* – a title that can be seen as a sort of ancestral Poet Laureate.

So in some ways he was even more at the centre of things than Chaucer. But he became a fierce opponent of Cardinal Wolsey, the most powerful figure on the scene for much of the time at Henry VIII's court, and it was Wolsey who, reacting against Skelton's torrent of scurrilousness, made him leave London for several years and take up a post as rector of a parish in south Norfolk.

Skelton's poems are full of satirical abuse, grotesqueness, energetic tumble and deliberately puzzling political obscurity. But he also wrote some very gentle and tender lyrics, several of them addressed to the Countess of Surrey and other aristocratic ladies, including one 'To Mistress Margaret Hussey' – playful, graceful, serene:

To Mistress Margaret Hussey

Merry Margaret
As midsummer flower,
Gentle as falcon
Or hawk of the tower:
With solace and gladness,
Much mirth and no madness,
All good and no badness;
So joyously,
So maidenly,
So womanly
Her demeaning
In every thing,
Far, far passing
That I can indite,
Or suffice to write
Of Merry Margaret
As midsummer flower
Gentle as falcon
Or hawk of the tower.
As patient and still
And as full of good will
As fair Isaphill,
Coriander,
Sweet pomander,
Good Cassander;
Steadfast of thought,
Well made, well wrought,
Far may be sought,
Ere that you can find
So courteous, so kind
As merry Margaret,
This midsummer flower,
Gentle as falcon
Or hawk of the tower.

Later in the reign of Henry VIII, another poet who got into even graver trouble than Skelton was Sir Thomas Wyatt – an aristocrat (unlike Skelton) who began his career at the age of twenty-one as Clerk of the King's Jewels and who went on many diplomatic missions, to France, Italy, Spain and Holland. Twice he was imprisoned by Henry (first after being implicated in the Anne Boleyn scandal, next on a treason charge

8. Sir Thomas Wyatt, after Hans Holbein.

9. This sixteenth-century view of the Piazza di S. Pietro would have been familiar to Wyatt, who travelled abroad on many diplomatic missions.

because he was an ally of Thomas Cromwell): twice he was pardoned and released. He managed to die of natural causes at the age of thirty-nine, unlike the poet–friend with whom he is often associated, Henry Howard, Earl of Surrey, who was executed in the Tower at the age of thirty.

Wyatt's travels in Italy put him in touch with Italian poetry, such as that of Petrarch and Ariosto, some of which Chaucer had come across a century and a half earlier. Wyatt both translated their work and learned from it in writing his own poems. He wrote many love-songs, particularly for the lute; but the most striking of all his poems has a sombre, sardonic, unlyrical note, and what sounds to us to be an extraordinarily modern ring. Its eroticism is more piercing and direct than one finds in most poems of so-called 'courtly love'. There is real feeling here, expressed with passionate realism – a kind of poetry not heard before in English:

They flee from me . . .

They flee from me, that sometime did me seek
　　With naked foot, stalking in my chamber.
I have seen them gentle, tame, and meek,
　　That now are wild, and do not remember
　　That sometime they put themselves in danger
　　　　To take bread at my hand; and now they range
　　　　Busily seeking with a continual change.

Thanked be fortune it hath been otherwise
　　Twenty times better; but once, in special,
In thin array, after a pleasant guise,
　　When her loose gown from her shoulders did fall,
　　And she me caught in her arms long and small,
　　　　Therewith all sweetly did me kiss
　　　　And softly said, 'Dear heart, how like you this?'

It was no dream; I lay broad waking:
　　But all is turned, thorough my gentleness,
Into a strange fashion of forsaking;
　　And I have leave to go of her goodness,
　　And she also to use newfangleness.
　　　　But since that I so kindly am served,
　　　　I would fain know what she hath deserved.

Sixteenth-century England – the England of Henry VIII and Mary and Elizabeth I – was by no means the 'Merrie England' some people have supposed. Apart from poverty, there were tribulations which could affect the rich and powerful as well: disease, including a wave of plagues, political and religious punishments, tortures and executions. As he waited in the death cell on the eve of his own execution (for his part in what is known as the 'Babington Conspiracy' against Queen Elizabeth), a young man about whom very little else is known, and from whom nothing else in verse survives, wrote his own elegy. Chidiock Tichborne was executed in 1586.

10. A putative portrait of Chidiock Tichborne who was executed for conspiracy.

Written the Night Before His Execution

My prime of youth is but a frost of cares;
My feast of joy is but a dish of pain;
My crop of corn is but a field of tares;
And all my good is but vain hope of gain;
My life is fled, and yet I saw no sun;
And now I live, and now my life is done.

The spring is past, and yet it hath not sprung;
The fruit is dead, and yet the leaves be green;
My youth is gone, and yet I am but young;
I saw the world, and yet I was not seen;
My thread is cut, and yet it is not spun;
And now I live, and now my life is done.

I sought my death, and found it in my womb,
I looked for life, and saw it was a shade,
I trod the earth and knew it was my tomb,
And now I die, and now I am but made:
The glass is full, and now my glass is run,
And now I live, and now my life is done.

Even supposed 'entertainments' – spectacles, dramatic masques and tableaux – could include grim matter reflecting the dangers and uncertainties of life. One example from many is by Thomas Nashe, a journalist, pamphleteer and hack-of-all-writing-trades, who wrote a lament for a piece called *Summer's Last Will and Testament*. He wrote it at a time of plague, and that is precisely what it is: 'Song in Time of Plague':

11. Thomas Nashe, journalist, pamphleteer, hack and poet.

Song in Time of Plague

Adieu, farewell earth's bliss!
This world uncertain is:
Fond are life's lustful joys,
Death proves them all but toys.
None from his darts can fly;
I am sick, I must die –
          Lord, have mercy on us!

Rich men, trust not in wealth,
Gold cannot buy you health;
Physic himself must fade;
All things to end are made;
The plague full swift goes by;
I am sick, I must die –
          Lord, have mercy on us!

12. Death portrayed in
a late fifteenth-century
English manuscript.

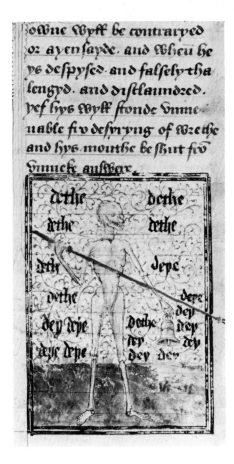

Beauty is but a flower
Which wrinkles will devour;
Brightness falls from the air;
Queens have died young and fair;
Dust hath closed Helen's eye;
I am sick, I must die –
      Lord, have mercy on us!

Strength stoops unto the grave,
Worms feed on Hector brave;
Swords may not fight with fate;
Earth still holds ope her gate;
Come, come! the bells do cry;
I am sick, I must die –
      Lord, have mercy on us!

Wit with his wantonness
Tasteth death's bitterness;
Hell's executioner
Hath no ears for to hear
What vain art can reply;
I am sick, I must die –
      Lord, have mercy on us!

Haste therefore each degree
To welcome destiny;
Heaven is our heritage,
Earth but a player's stage.
Mount we unto the sky;
I am sick, I must die –
      Lord, have mercy on us!

The idea in Nashe's poem of everything passing, of the decay of beauty
and wealth and power, is put more fiercely, even politically, in a poem
which was almost certainly, but not definitely, written by one of the great
men of the Elizabethan age, Sir Walter Raleigh – great not just as a writer
but as a statesman, soldier, explorer, adventurer. He was twice disgraced
and imprisoned, first by Queen Elizabeth, finally by James I, at whose
orders he was executed on the ludicrous charge that he was an 'agent of
Spain'. His poem, 'The Lie', is a lively, bitter, dignified and stoical homily
on the necessity of being honest:

13. Sir Walter Raleigh
painted by Nicholas
Hilliard c. 1585.

The Lie

Go, soul, the body's guest,
  Upon a thankless arrant;
Fear not to touch the best;
  The truth shall be thy warrant.
    Go, since I needs must die,
    And give the world the lie.

Say to the court, it glows
  And shines like rotten wood;
Say to the church, it shows
  What's good, and doth no good:
    If church and court reply,
    Then give them both the lie.

Tell potentates, they live
  Acting by other's action,
Not loved unless they give,
  Not strong but by affection:
    If potentates reply,
    Give potentates the lie.

Tell men of high condition
That manage the estate,
Their purpose is ambition,
Their practice only hate:
And if they once reply,
Then give them all the lie.

Tell them that brave it most,
They beg for more by spending,
Who, in their greatest cost,
Seek nothing but commending:
And if they make reply,
Then give them all the lie.

Tell zeal it wants devotion;
Tell love it is but lust;
Tell time it metes but motion;
Tell flesh it is but dust:
And wish them not reply,
For thou must give the lie.

Tell age it daily wasteth;
Tell honour how it alters;
Tell beauty how she blasteth;
Tell favour how it falters:
And as they shall reply,
Give every one the lie.

Tell wit how much it wrangles
In tickle points of niceness;
Tell wisdom she entangles
Herself in over-wiseness:
And when they do reply,
Straight give them both the lie.

Tell physic of her boldness;
Tell skill it is prevention;
Tell charity of coldness;
Tell law it is contention:
And as they do reply,
So give them still the lie.

Tell fortune of her blindness;
  Tell nature of decay;
Tell friendship of unkindness;
  Tell justice of delay:
    And if they will reply,
    Then give them all the lie.

Tell arts they have no soundness,
  But vary by esteeming;
Tell schools they want profoundness,
  And stand too much on seeming:
    If arts and schools reply,
    Give arts and schools the lie.

Tell faith it's fled the city;
  Tell how the country erreth;
Tell, manhood shakes off pity;
  Tell, virtue least preferreth:
    And if they do reply,
    Spare not to give the lie.

So when thou hast, as I
  Commanded thee, done blabbing,
Although to give the lie
  Deserves no less than stabbing,
    Stab at thee he that will,
    No stab thy soul can kill.

The world on which Raleigh throws contempt, the world of jockeying for position, and frustrated ambition, and intrigue, was also very much the world of Christopher Marlowe, who came from a humble background (his father was a Canterbury cobbler) but who fought his way up the ladder by means of cleverness and drive. Not only was Marlowe already a successful playwright in his twenties, writing such plays as *Tamburlaine* and *Dr Faustus* for two London companies: he was also obscurely involved in government service, as an agent or even a double-agent, and he always lived – as he died – on the dangerous edge of things, being summoned before the Privy Council for alleged sedition and blasphemy. At the age of twenty-nine Marlowe was stabbed to death in a tavern brawl in London,

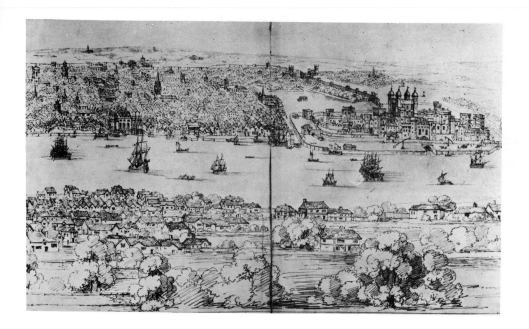

14. (above) Thames-side London and the Tower c. 1555 by Anthony van den Wyngaerde.

15. (right) A putative portrait dated 1585 of Christopher Marlow aged about 21, when he had already written *Tamburlaine the Great*.

16. (opposite) 'The shepherd swains shall dance and sing For thy delight each May morning.'

an incident which was hushed up as being an argument over money but which was much more likely something to do with his activities as a spy. Yet it would be hard to guess any such thing from his elegant and courtly little pastoral lyric, 'The Passionate Shepherd to His Love':

The Passionate Shepherd to His Love

Come live with me and be my Love,
And we will all the pleasures prove
That hills and valleys, dales and fields,
Or woods or steepy mountains yields.

And we will sit upon the rocks,
And see the shepherds feed their flocks
By shallow rivers, to whose falls
Melodious birds sing madrigals.

And I will make thee beds of roses
And a thousand fragrant posies;
A cap of flowers, and a kirtle
Embroider'd all with leaves of myrtle.

A gown made of the finest wool
Which from our pretty lambs we pull;
Fair-lined slippers for the cold,
With buckles of the purest gold.

A belt of straw and ivy-buds
With coral clasps and amber studs:
And if these pleasures may thee move,
Come live with me and be my Love.

The shepherd swains shall dance and sing
For thy delight each May morning:
If these delights thy mind may move,
Then live with me and be my Love.

The Elizabethan age was the great age of the sonnet – fourteen-line
poems originally following Italian models, and often combined in groups
or sequences concerned with or addressed to a loved one. Sir Philip
Sidney – another soldier–courtier poet like Raleigh – wrote many of

17. Sir Philip Sidney,
soldier, courtier and
poet, by an unknown
artist.

them. His sequence, *Astrophel and Stella*, consists of over a hundred sonnets, together with some songs. Addressed to 'Stella' ('She, dear She'), they are smooth, mellifluous even, and are technically perhaps the most perfect poems which had yet been written in English. One of the best-known sonnets in the sequence uses the image of the moon; another is an address to sleep:

> Come, sleep, O sleep, the certain knot of peace,
> The baiting place of wit, the balm of woe,
> The poor man's wealth, the prisoner's release,
> Th'indifferent judge between the high and low;
> With shield of proof shield me from out the prease
> Of those fierce darts despair at me doth throw;
> O make me in those civil wars to cease;
> I will good tribute pay, if thou do so.
> Take thou of me smooth pillows, sweetest bed,
> A chamber deaf to noise and blind to light,
> A rosy garland and a weary head;
> And if these things, as being thine by right,
> Move not thy heavy grace, thou shalt in me,
> Livelier than elsewhere, Stella's image see.

Edmund Spenser also wrote a sonnet sequence, *Amoretti*, as well as two great marriage hymns ('Epithalamion' and 'Prothalamion') and much else. But Spenser's large-scale achievement is his huge allegorical pageant, *The Faerie Queene*. He intended it to have twelve books, but in fact there are only seven, and even the seventh is unfinished and detached from the rest. The whole thing was explained by Spenser himself as intended to be a 'continued allegory or dark conceit'; and he also said that its framework was that of 'the twelve moral virtues as Aristotle hath devised'. The result of both intentions is a national patriotic vision of Love, Friendship, Beauty and Courage, as exemplified in the person of the Queen herself, Elizabeth I.

But within and beside this run a whole series of loosely connected or almost entirely unconnected moral adventures and situations, many of them with quite specific contemporary references to be read underneath the 'dark conceit'. It is a very literary poem, full of conscious archaisms and harkings-back, both in language and in plot, and it moves throughout on an exalted level.

18. Edmund Spenser painted by Benjamin Wilson.

One of the sections of *The Faerie Queene* which can be detached from the rest without doing real damage is the description of the Bower of Bliss in Book Two. The central character in this book is Sir Guyon, and the moral virtue is Temperance. One of the tempting places that Sir Guyon subdues, with the help of an Elf and a Palmer (that is, a poor wandering monk), is this erotic paradise, where they find a wanton Lady and her lover, whom they tie up:

from The Faerie Queen, Book Two

Eftsoones they heard a most melodious sound,
    Of all that mote delight a daintie eare,
    Such as attonce might not on liuing ground,
    Saue in this Paradise, be heard elsewhere:
    Right hard it was, for wight, which did it heare,

To read, what manner musicke that mote bee:
For all that pleasing is to liuing eare,
Was there consorted in one harmonee,
Birdes, voyces, instruments, windes, waters, all agree.

The ioyous birdes shrouded in chearefull shade,
   Their notes vnto the voyce attempred sweet;
   Th'Angelicall soft trembling voyces made
   To th'instruments diuine respondence meet:
   The siluer sounding instruments did meet
   With the base murmure of the waters fall:
   The waters fall with difference discreet,
   Now soft, now loud, vnto the wind did call:
The gentle warbling wind low answered to all.

There, whence that Musick seemed heard to bee,
   Was the fair Witch her selfe now solacing,
   With a new Louer, whom through sorceree
   And witchcraft, she from farre did thither bring:
   There she had him now layd a slombering,
   In secret shade, after long wanton joyes:
   Whilst round about them pleasauntly did sing
   Many faire Ladies, and lasciuious boyes,
That euer mixt their song with light licentious toyes.

And all that while, right ouer him she hong,
   With her false eyes fast fixed in his sight,
   As seeking medicine, whence she was stong,
   Or greedily depasturing delight:
   And oft inclining downe with kisses light,
   For feare of waking him, his lips bedewd,
   And through his humid eyes did sucke his spright,
   Quite molten into lust and pleasure lewd;
Wherewith she sighed soft, as if his case she rewd.

The whiles some one did chaunt this louely lay;
   Ah see, who so faire thing doest faine to see,
   In springing flowre the image of thy day;
   Ah see the Virgin Rose, how sweetly shee
   Doth first peepe forth with bashfull modestee,
   That fairer seemes, the lesse ye see her may;
   Lo see soone after how more bold and free
   Her baréd bosome she doth broad display;
Loe see soone after, how she fades, and falles away.

So passeth, in the passing of a day,
    Of mortall life the leafe, the bud, the flowre,
    Ne more doth flourish after first decay,
    That earst was sought to decke both bed and bowre,
    Of many a ladie, and many a Paramowre:
    Gather therefore the Rose of loue, whilest yet is
       prime,
    For soone comes age, that will her pride deflowre:
    Gather the Rose of loue, whilest yet is time,
While louing thou mayst loued be with equall crime.

He ceast, and then gan all the quire of birdes
    Their diuerse notes t'attune vnto his lay,
    As in approuance of his pleasing words.
    The constant paire heard all, that he did say,
    Yet swarued not, but kept their forward way,
    Through many couert groues, and thickets close,
    In which they creeping did at last display
    That wanton Ladie, with her louer lose,
Whose sleepie head she in her lap did soft dispose.

Vpon a bed of Roses she was layd,
    As faint through heat, or dight to pleasant sin,
    And was arayd, or rather disarayd,
    All in a vele of silke and siluer thin,
    That hid no whit her alabaster skin,
    But rather shewd more white, if more might bee:
    More subtile web Arachne cannot spin,
    Nor the fine nets, which oft we wouen see
Of scorched deaw, do not in th'aire more lightly flee.

Her snowy brest was bare to readie spoyle
    Of hungry eies, which n'ote therewith be fild,
    And yet through langvour of her late sweet toyle,
    Few drops, more cleare then Nectar, forth distild,
    That like pure Orient perles adowne it trild
    And her fair eyes sweet smyling in delight,
    Moystened their fierie beames, with which she thrild
    Fraile harts, yet quenched not; like starry light
Which sparckling on the silent waues, does seeme more
    bright.

The young man sleeping by her, seemd to bee
    Some goodly swayne of honorable place,
    That certes it great pittie was to see
    Him his nobilitie so foule deface;
    A sweet regard, and amiable grace,
    Mixed with manly sternnesse did appeare
    Yet sleeping, in his well proportiond face,
    And on his tender lips the downy heare
Did now but freshly spring, and silken blossomes beare.

His warlike armes, the idle instruments
    Of sleeping praise, were hong vpon a tree,
    And his braue shield, full of old moniments,
    Was fowly ra'st, that none the signes might see;
    Ne for them, ne for honour cared hee,
    Ne ought, that did to his aduauncement tend,
    But in lewd loues, and wastfull luxuree,
    His dayes, his goods, his bodie he did spend:
O horrible enchantment, that him so did blend.

The noble Elfe, and carefull Palmer drew
    So nigh them, minding nought, but lustfull game,
    That sudden forth they on them rusht, and threw
    A subtile net, which onely for the same
    The skilfull Palmer formally did frame.
    So held them vnder fast, the whiles the rest
    Fled all away for feare of fowler shame.
    The faire Enchauntresse, so vnwares opprest,
Tryde all her arts, and all her sleights, thence out to
        wrest.

And eke her louer stroue: but all in vaine;
    For that same net so cunningly was wound,
    That neither guile, nor force might it distraine.
    They tooke them both, and both them strongly bound
    In captiue bandes, which there they readie found:
    But her in chaines of adamant he tyde;
    For nothing else might keepe her safe and sound;
    But Verdant (so he hight) he soone vntyde,
And counsell sage insteed thereof to him applyde.

But all those pleasant bowres and Pallace braue,
Guyon broke downe, with rigour pittilesse;
Ne ought their goodly workmanship might saue
Them from the tempest of his wrathfulnesse,
But that their blisse he turn'd to balefulnesse:
Their groues he feld, their gardins did deface,
Their arbers spoyle, their Cabinets suppresse,
Their banket houses burne, their buildings race,
And of the fairest late, now made the fowlest place.

19. A posthumous picture of Michael Drayton attributed to the English painter and engraver George Vertue.

Much of Spenser may seem remote and artificial to people today, and it may be we feel something more direct and striking in some sonnets by his younger contemporary, Michael Drayton. Drayton wrote copiously, constantly revising his work throughout his long life. From all his sonnets, here is just one, a late piece (written in 1619) from a sequence called *Idea*: a poem of regretful lovers parting, at the end of their affair:

The Parting

Since there's no help, come let us kiss and part –
Nay, I have done, you get no more of me;
And I am glad, yea, glad with all my heart,
That thus so cleanly I myself can free.
Shake hands for ever, cancel all our vows,
And when we meet at any time again,
Be it not seen in either of our brows
That we one jot of former love retain.
Now at the last gasp of Love's latest breath,
When, his pulse failing, Passion speechless lies,
When Faith is kneeling by his bed of death,
And Innocence is closing up his eyes,
    – Now if thou wouldst, when all have given him
      over,
    From death to life thou might'st him yet recover.

But the most famous sonnets of the Elizabethan age are by a young man who was about to become the dominant playwright not only of his own time but through all succeeding ages, and not only in England but throughout the world: William Shakespeare. Shakespeare's 152 sonnets were first published together in 1609, but they were probably written in the 1590s, when he was in his late twenties.

They seem to divide into two main groups. Sonnets 1 to 126 are addressed to, or have as their subject, a young man much loved by him and much superior to him socially; while sonnets 127 to 152 concern his mingled love and loathing for a 'dark lady' who, having already had an affair with the poet, has now seduced the young man. But all biographical investigations, and most 'explanations', rapidly run into difficulties. For all the confident assertions of many commentators, the identities and the truths or fictions of the sonnets' 'characters' will never be established.

I have chosen five of these powerful and enigmatic poems, four of them from the first group, and ending with number 129 – a grim, remorseless meditation on sexual lust:

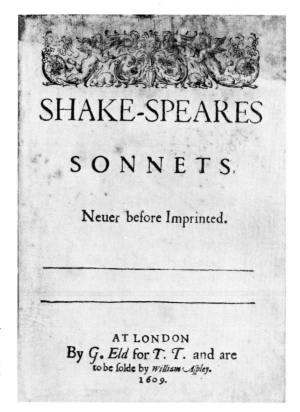

SHAKE-SPEARES

SONNETS.

Neuer before Imprinted.

AT LONDON
By G. *Eld* for *T. T.* and are
to be folde by *William Apley.*
1609.

20. The title page of the 1609 volume, *Shakespeare's Sonnets,* the first time his 152 sonnets were published together.

18

Shall I compare thee to a Summers day?
Thou art more lovely and more temperate:
Rough windes do shake the darling buds of Maie,
And Sommers lease hath all too short a date:
Sometime too hot the eye of heaven shines,
And often is his gold complexion dimm'd,
And every faire from faire some-time declines,
By chance, or natures changing course untrim'd:
But thy eternall Sommer shall not fade,
Nor loose possession of that faire thou ow'st,
Nor shall death brag thou wandr'st in his shade,
When in eternall lines to time thou grow'st,
    So long as men can breath or eyes can see,
    So long lives this, and this gives life to thee.

29

When in disgrace with Fortune and mens eyes,
I all alone beweepe my out-cast state,
And trouble deafe heaven with my bootlesse cries,
And looke upon my selfe and curse my fate.
Wishing me like to one more rich in hope,
Featur'd like him, like him with friends possest,
Desiring this mans art, and that mans skope,
With what I most injoy contented least,
Yet in these thoughts my selfe almost despising,
Haplye I thinke on thee, and then my state,
(Like to the Larke at breake of daye arising)
From sullen earth sings himns at Heavens gate,
    For thy sweet love remembred such welth brings,
    That then I skorne to change my state with Kings.

94

They that have powre to hurt, and will doe none,
That doe not do the thing, they most do showe,
Who moving others, are themselves as stone,
Unmooved, cold, and to temptation slow:
They rightly do inherrit heavens graces,
And husband natures ritches from expence,
They are the Lords and owners of their faces,
Others, but stewards of their excellence:
The sommers flowre is to the sommer sweet,
Though to it selfe, it onely live and die,
But if that flowre with base infection meete,
The basest weed out-braves his dignity:
    For sweetest things turne sowrest by their deedes,
    Lillies that fester, smell far worse than weeds.

116

Let me not to the marriage of true mindes
Admit impediments, love is not love
Which alters when it alteration findes,
Or bends with the remover to remove.
O no, it is an ever fixed marke
That lookes on tempests and is never shaken;
It is the star to every wandring barke,
Whose worths unknowne, although his higth be taken.
Lov's not Times foole, though rosie lips and cheeks
Within his bending sickles compasse come,
Love alters not with his breefe houres and weekes,
But bears it out even to the edge of doome:
    If this be error and upon me proved,
    I never writ, nor no man ever loved.

129

Th'expence of Spirit in a waste of shame
Is lust in action, and till action, lust
Is perjurd, murdrous, blouddy, full of blame,
Savage, extreame, rude, cruell, not to trust,
Injoyd no sooner but dispised straight,
Past reason hunted, and no sooner had
Past reason hated as a swollowed bayt,
On purpose layd to make the taker mad.
Mad in pursut and in possession so,
Had, having, and in quest, to have extreame,
A blisse in proofe and provd a very wo,
Before, a joy proposd, behind, a dreame,
    All this the world well knowes yet none knowes well,
    To shun the heaven that leads men to this hell.

THREE

Shakespeare
1564-1616

Our poesy is as a gum, which oozes
From whence 'tis nourished: the fire i' the flint
Shows not till it be struck; our gentle flame
Provokes itself, and, like the current flies
Each bound it chafes . . .

With these words, spoken by a minor character in one of his less familiar plays – the Poet in *Timon of Athens* – Shakespeare conjures up a brilliant, partly ironical image of the poetic process. The fire of Shakespeare's poetry was struck from the flint of circumstance: that is to say, he was a hard-working, prolific writer of plays (well over thirty plays in twenty years), whose genius was harnessed to producing successful public entertainments. His sonnets and his other non-dramatic poems, such as *Venus and Adonis* and *The Phoenix and the Turtle*, are great, certainly. But the only proper way to show his genius in miniature is to show it in action in the plays. Impossible though such mini-anthologising of Shakespeare is, I have tried to pluck out a few brief moments in some of the greatest plays, to show in chronological order his variety over the years in many moods.

Though he began as a writer of history plays (the three parts of *Henry VI*), Shakespeare also wrote both tragedy and comedy early in his career, probably by the time he was thirty. Already in *Romeo and Juliet* he combines both. This story of family feud in Verona (between Capulets and Montagues) and passionate young love is relieved and lightened as soon as Juliet's nurse appears – that prattling, bawdy, warm-hearted woman who loves her Juliet and who loves life:

from Romeo and Juliet

Nurse. Even or odd, of all days in the year,
Come Lammas-eve at night shall she be fourteen.
Susan and she – God rest all Christian souls! –
Were of an age. Well, Susan is with God;
She was too good for me. But, as I said,

On Lammas-eve at night shall she be fourteen;
That shall she, marry; I remember it well.
'Tis since the earthquake now eleven years;
And she was wean'd, I never shall forget it,
Of all the days of the year, upon that day;
For I had then laid wormwood to my dug,
Sitting in the sun under the dove-house wall;
My lord and you were then at Mantua.
Nay, I do bear a brain: – but, as I said,
When it did taste the wormwood on the nipple
Of my dug and felt it bitter, pretty fool!
To see it tetchy and fall out with the dug.
'Shake,' quoth the dove-house: 'twas no need, I trow,
To bid me trudge:
And since that time it is eleven years;
For then she could stand high lone; nay, by the rood,
She could have run and waddled all about;
For even the day before she broke her brow:
And then my husband – God be with his soul!
A' was a merry man – took up the child:
'Yea,' quoth he, 'dost thou fall upon thy face?
Thou wilt fall backward when thou hast more wit;
Wilt thou not, Jule?' and, by my halidom,
The pretty wretch left crying, and said 'Ay.'
To see now how a jest shall come about!
I warrant, an I should live a thousand years,
I never should forget it: 'Wilt thou not, Jule?' quoth he;
And, pretty fool, it stinted and said 'Ay.'
　　Lady Capulet. Enough of this; I pray thee, hold thy
　　　　peace.
　　Nurse. Yes, madam. Yet I cannot choose but laugh,
To think it should leave crying, and say 'Ay.'
And yet, I warrant, it had upon its brow
A bump as big as a young cockerel's stone;
A parlous knock; and it cried bitterly:
'Yea,' quoth my husband, 'fall'st upon thy face?
Thou wilt fall backward when thou com'st to age;
Wilt thou not, Jule?' it stinted and said 'Ay.'
　　Jul. And stint thou too, I pray thee, nurse say I.
　　Nurse. Peace, I have done. God mark thee to his
　　　　grace!
Thou wast the prettiest babe that e'er I nursed;
An I might live to see thee married once,
I have my wish.

21. The only portrait of Shakespeare
believed to have been painted from life,
by an unknown artist.

Shakespeare's theatre, the Elizabethan theatre, was not a place in
which realism could be easily established: often open to the sky, with very
rudimentary props, and without any of the illusionary tricks which we

Convent garden   S. Clement

Arundel house

Fox house   Temple stayrs

Temple

Black fryars

The Globe

Beere bayting

22. (above) The Globe Theatre,
where Shakespeare's plays were
performed, on the south bank of
the Thames.

23. (below) The Swan an
Elizabethan theatre like the
Globe, drawn by Jan de Witte
in 1596, showing the stage open
to the sky.

tectum

porticus

orchestra

mimorum
ædes

proscenium

planities siue arena

have grown used to in the modern theatre, and indeed in films and on television. Words had to do most of the work – in setting the scene, for example. This is a problem Shakespeare tackles head-on in his opening chorus to *Henry V* – a marvellous bid to convince the audience that the limitations of the theatre are not really limitations at all:

from Henry V

O! for a Muse of fire, that would ascend
The brightest heaven of invention;
A kingdom for a stage, princes to act
And monarchs to behold the swelling scene.
Then should the war-like Harry, like himself,
Assume the port of Mars; and at his heels,
Leash'd in like hounds, should famine, sword, and fire
Crouch for employment. But pardon, gentles all,
The flat unraised spirits that hath dar'd
On this unworthy scaffold to bring forth
So great an object: can this cockpit hold
The vasty fields of France? or may we cram
Within this wooden O the very casques
That did affright the air at Agincourt?
O, pardon! since a crooked figure may
Attest in little place a million;
And let us, ciphers to this great accompt,
On your imaginary forces work.
Suppose within the girdle of these walls
Are now confin'd two mighty monarchies,
Whose high upreared and abutting fronts
The perilous narrow ocean parts asunder:
Piece out our imperfections with your thoughts:
Into a thousand parts divide one man,
And make imaginary puissance;
Think when we talk of horses that you see them
Printing their proud hoofs i' the receiving earth;
For 'tis your thoughts that now must deck our kings,
Carry them here and there, jumping o'er times,
Turning the accomplishment of many years
Into an hour-glass: for the which supply,
Admit me Chorus to this history;
Who prologue-like your humble patience pray,
Gently to hear, kindly to judge, our play.

Among Shakespeare's twelve comedies, *Twelfth Night* has always been one of the most popular. But in fact what is sometimes forgotten is that, particularly in the comedies and most of all in *Twelfth Night* and *Much Ado About Nothing*, some of the best and most characteristic Shakespeare is written in prose – over 60 per cent of *Twelfth Night*, over 70 per cent of *Much Ado*. . . . Sir Toby Belch, Sir Andrew Aguecheek and elsewhere in Shakespeare much of what Shylock says, much of Benedick and Beatrice, all of Falstaff – all these characters speak in prose. So they cannot really be represented in a book of English verse. But one of the most delicate scenes in *Twelfth Night* shows Shakespeare's verse at its gentlest – the moment when Viola, in her male disguise as Cesario, is left with the Duke Orsino and obliquely suggests her love for him:

from Twelfth Night

Duke. Once more, Cesario,
Get thee to yond same sovereign cruelty:
Tell her, my love, more noble than the world,
Prizes not quantity of dirty lands;
The parts that fortune hath bestow'd upon her,
Tell her, I hold as giddily as fortune;
But 'tis that miracle and queen of gems
That nature pranks her in attracts my soul.
    Viola. But if she cannot love you, sir?
    Duke. I cannot be so answer'd.
    Viola.   Sooth, but you must.
Say that some lady, as perhaps, there is,
Hath for your love as great a pang of heart
As you have for Olivia: you cannot love her;
You tell her so; must she not then be answer'd?
    Duke. There is no woman's sides
Can bide the beating of so strong a passion
As love doth give my heart; no woman's heart
So big, to hold so much; they lack retention.
Alas! their love may be call'd appetite,
No motion of the liver, but the palate,
That suffer surfeit, cloyment and revolt;
But mine is all as hungry as the sea,
And can digest as much. Make no compare
Between that love a woman can bear me
And that I owe Olivia.
    Viola.   Ay, but I know, –
    Duke. What dost thou know?

Viola. Too well what love women to men may owe:
In faith, they are as true of heart as we.
My father had a daughter lov'd a man,
As it might be, perhaps, were I a woman,
I should your lordship.
    Duke.   And what's her history?
    Viola. A blank, my lord. She never told her love,
But let concealment, like a worm i' the bud,
Feed on her damask cheek: she pin'd in thought,
And with a green and yellow melancholy,
She sat like Patience on a monument,
Smiling at grief. Was not this love indeed?
We men may say more, swear more; but indeed
Our shows are more than will, for still we prove
Much in our vows, but little in our love.
    Duke. But died thy sister of her love, my boy?
    Viola. I am all the daughters of my father's house,
And all the brothers too; and yet I know not.
Sir, shall I to this lady?
    Duke.   Ay, that's the theme.
To her in haste; give her this jewel; say
My love can give no place, bide no denay.

Shakespeare wrote his five or six greatest tragedies in the early years of the seventeenth century. Of them all, it is probably *Hamlet* that has most haunted the imagination of the world – particularly in the soliloquies, those moments of self-communion when (as the early nineteenth-century critic Hazlitt put it) 'they are as real as our own thoughts . . . It is *we* who are Hamlet'. There is, for example, that moment when Hamlet sits alone, brooding on his father's death and his mother's 'o'er-hasty marriage':

from Hamlet

Hamlet. O! that this too too solid flesh would melt,
Thaw and resolve itself into a dew;
Or that the Everlasting had not fix'd
His canon 'gainst self-slaughter! O God! O God!
How weary, stale, flat, and unprofitable
Seem to me all the uses of this world.
Fie on't! O fie! 'tis an unweeded garden,
That grows to seed; things rank and gross in nature
Possess it merely. That it should come to this!
But two months dead: nay, not so much, not two:

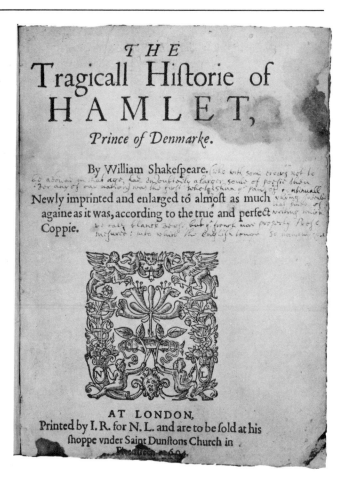

24. The title page of the 1604 edition of *Hamlet*.

So excellent a king; that was, to this,
Hyperion to a satyr; so loving to my mother
That he might not beteem the winds of heaven
Visit her face too roughly. Heaven and earth!
Must I remember? why, she would hang on him,
As if increase of appetite had grown
By what it fed on; and yet, within a month,
Let me not think on't: Frailty, thy name is woman!
A little month; or ere those shoes were old
With which she follow'd my poor father's body,
Like Niobe, all tears; why she, even she, –
O God! a beast, that wants discourse of reason,
Would have mourn'd longer, – married with mine uncle,
My father's brother, but no more like my father
Than I to Hercules: within a month,

Ere yet the salt of most unrighteous tears
Had left the flushing in her galled eyes,
She married. O! most wicked speed, to post
With such dexterity to incestuous sheets.
It is not nor it cannot come to good;
But break, my heart, for I must hold my tongue!

One of Shakespeare's subtlest gifts is the way in which he can reveal a character through a speech which is also a piece of story-telling, a recounting of a series of memories. There is that moment in *Othello*, for instance, when Othello himself is called on by the Duke to explain to the Senators of Venice whether he indeed made Desdemona fall in love with him through using spells or witchcraft. What follows is a marvellously poised and persuasive piece of rhetoric by a man who describes himself as 'rude' in his speech 'and little blessed with the soft phrase of peace':

from Othello

Othello. Her father lov'd me; oft invited me;
Still question'd me the story of my life
From year to year, the battles, sieges, fortunes
That I have pass'd.
I ran it through, even from my boyish days
To the very moment that he bade me tell it;
Wherein I spake of most disastrous chances,
Of moving accidents by flood and field,
Of hair-breadth 'scapes i' the imminent deadly breach,
Of being taken by the insolent foe
And sold to slavery, of my redemption thence
And portance in my travel's history;
Wherein of antres vast and desarts idle,
Rough quarries, rocks and hills whose heads touch
    heaven,
It was my hint to speak, such was the process;
And of the Cannibals that each other eat,
The Anthropophagi, and men whose heads
Do grow beneath their shoulders. This to hear
Would Desdemona seriously incline;
But still the house-affairs would draw her thence;
Which ever as she could with haste dispatch,
She'd come again, and with a greedy ear
Devour up my discourse. Which I observing,
Took once a pliant hour, and found good means

To draw from her a prayer of earnest heart
That I would all my pilgrimage dilate,
Whereof by parcels she had something heard,
But not intentively: I did consent;
And often did beguile her of her tears,
When I did speak of some distressful stroke
That my youth suffer'd. My story being done,
She gave me for my pains a world of sighs:
She swore, in faith, 'twas strange, 'twas passing strange;
'Twas pitiful, 'twas wondrous pitiful:
She wish'd she had not heard it, yet she wish'd
That heaven had made her such a man; she thank'd me,
And bade me, if I had a friend that lov'd her,
I should but teach him how to tell my story,
And that would woo her. Upon this hint I spake:
She lov'd me for the dangers I had pass'd,
And I lov'd her that she did pity them.
This only is the witchcraft I have us'd:
Here comes the lady; let her witness it.

Some of the most poignant moments in Shakespeare are moments of recognition or reconciliation, moments when conflict is resolved or misunderstanding becomes understanding. Such moments seem to come particularly in the later plays, but not only in the late 'Romances': earlier, there is the scene in *King Lear*, at the end of Act 4, when Cordelia, Lear's estranged daughter, speaks to him as he slowly emerges from humiliation and madness, cast out by Cordelia's cruel older sisters, Goneril and Regan, into the storm:

from King Lear

Cordelia. He wakes; speak to him.
Doctor. Madam, do you; 'tis fittest.
Cordelia. How does my royal lord? How fares your
 majesty?
Lear. You do me wrong to take me out o' the grave;
Thou art a soul in bliss; but I am bound
Upon a wheel of fire, that mine own tears
Do scald like molten lead.
Cordelia.   Sir, do you know me?
Lear. You are a spirit, I know; when did you die?
Cordelia. Still, still, far wide.
Doctor. He's scarce awake; let him alone awhile.

M. VVilliam Shake-fpeare,
HIS
True Chronicle Hiſtory of the life
and death of King *Lear*, and his
three Daughters.

With the vnfortunate life of E D G A R,
ſonne and heire to the Earle of *Gloceſter*, and
his ſullen and aſſumed humour of T O M
of Bedlam.

As it was plaid before the Kings Maieſty at White-Hall, vp-
pon S. Stephens night, in Chriſtmas Hollidaies.

By his Maieſties Seruants, playing vſually at the
Globe on the *Banck-ſide*.

Printed for *Nathaniel Butter*.
1608.

25. The title page of
King Lear, published in
1608.

Lear. Where have I been? Where am I? Fair day-light?
I am mightily abus'd. I should even die with pity
To see another thus. I know not what to say.
I will not swear these are my hands: let's see;
I feel this pin prick. Would I were assur'd
Of my condition!
   Cordelia.   O! look upon me, sir,
And hold your hands in benediction o'er me.
No, sir, you must not kneel.
   Lear.   Pray, do not mock me:
I am a very foolish fond old man,
Fourscore and upward, not an hour more or less:
And, to deal plainly,
I fear I am not in my perfect mind.
Methinks I should know you and know this man;
Yet I am doubtful: for I am mainly ignorant
What place this is, and all the skill I have
Remembers not these garments; nor I know not
Where I did lodge last night. Do not laugh at me;
For, as I am a man, I think this lady
To be my child Cordelia.

Cordelia.   And so I am, I am.
Lear. Be your tears wet? Yes, faith. I pray, weep not:
If you have poison for me, I will drink it.
I know you do not love me; for your sisters
Have, as I do remember, done me wrong:
You have some cause, they have not.
     Cordelia.   No cause, no cause.
     Lear. Am I in France?
     Kent.   In your own kingdom, sir.
     Lear. Do not abuse me.
     Doctor. Be comforted, good madam; the great rage,
You see, is kill'd in him; and yet it is danger
To make him even o'er the time he has lost.
Desire him to go in; trouble him no more
Till further settling.
     Cordelia. Will't please your highness walk?
     Lear.   You must bear with me.
Pray you now, forget and forgive: I am old and foolish.

A number of Shakespeare's finest, most memorable speeches are given to minor characters. In *Antony and Cleopatra*, Enobarbus, one of Mark Antony's friends, is in many ways a comic character, certainly a lightweight one. As with the majority of Shakespeare's less serious figures, most of the time he speaks in prose. But there is an extraordinary passage in which, describing Cleopatra's meeting with Antony to two of Caesar's companions, Enobarbus suddenly surprises us with a vivid, sensuous and at the same time slightly mocking speech in verse: a passage that, over 300 years later, T. S. Eliot was to parody or make play with in *The Waste Land*, as we shall see in a later section of this book:

from Antony and Cleopatra

Enobarbus.
The barge she sat in, like a burnish'd throne,
Burn'd on the water; the poop was beaten gold,
Purple the sails, and so perfumed, that
The winds were love-sick with them, the oars were
     silver,
Which to the tune of flutes kept stroke, and made
The water which they beat to follow faster,
As amorous of their strokes. For her own person,
It beggar'd all description; she did lie
In her pavilion, – cloth-of-gold of tissue, –
O'er-picturing that Venus where we see

The fancy outwork nature; on each side her
Stood pretty-dimpled boys, like smiling Cupids,
With divers-colour'd fans, whose wind did seem
To glow the delicate cheeks which they did cool,
And what they undid did.
    Agrippa.   O! rare for Antony.
    Enobarbus. Her gentlewomen, like the Nereides,
So many mermaids, tended her i' the eyes,
And made their bends adornings; at the helm
A seeming mermaid steers; the silken tackle
Swell with the touches of those flower-soft hands,
That yarely frame the office. From the barge
A strange invisible perfume hits the sense
Of the adjacent wharfs. The city cast
Her people out upon her, and Antony,
Enthron'd i' the market-place, did sit alone,
Whistling to the air; which, but for vacancy,
Had gone to gaze on Cleopatra too
And made a gap in nature.
    Agrippa.   Rare Egyptian!
    Enobarbus. Upon her landing, Antony sent to her,
Invited her to supper; she replied
It should be better he became her guest,
Which she entreated. Our courteous Antony,
Whom ne'er the word of 'No' woman heard speak,
Being barber'd ten times o'er, goes to the feast,
And, for his ordinary pays his heart
For what his eyes eat only.
    Agrippa.   Royal wench!
She made great Caesar lay his sword to bed;
He plough'd her, and she cropp'd.
    Enobarbus.   I saw her once
Hop forty paces through the public street;
And having lost her breath, she spoke, and panted
That she did make defect perfection,
And, breathless, power breathe forth.
    Mecenas. Now Antony must leave her utterly.
    Enobarbus. Never; he will not:
Age cannot wither her, nor custom stale
Her infinite variety; other women cloy
The appetites they feed, but she makes hungry
Where most she satisfies; for vilest things
Become themselves in her, that the holy priests
Bless her when she is riggish.

Songs play a significant part in Shakespeare's verse – very often songs which sum up, or comment ironically on, a theme in the drama. Or a song may sometimes serve as a moment of punctuation – as in one of his last plays, *Cymbeline*, when the two princes, Guiderius and Arviragus, pronounce a dirge or funeral song over the supposedly dead body of their sister Imogen:

from Cymbeline

Guiderius.	Fear no more the heat o' the sun,
	Nor the furious winter's rages;
	Thou thy worldly task hast done,
	Home art gone, and ta'en thy wages;
	Golden lads and girls all must,
	As chimney-sweepers, come to dust.
Arviragus.	Fear no more the frown o' the great,
	Thou art past the tyrant's stroke:
	Care no more to clothe and eat;
	To thee the reed is as the oak;
	The sceptre, learning, physic, must
	All follow this, and come to dust.
Guiderius.	Fear no more the lightning-flash,
Arviragus.	Nor the all-dreaded thunder-stone;
Guiderius.	Fear not slander, censure rash;
Arviragus.	Thou hast finish'd joy and moan:
Both.	All lovers young, all lovers must
	Consign to thee, and come to dust.
Guiderius.	No exorciser harm thee!
Arviragus.	Nor no witchcraft charm thee!
Guiderius.	Ghost unlaid forbear thee!
Arviragus.	Nothing ill come near thee!
Both.	Quiet consummation have;
	And renowned be thy grave!

Though Shakespeare did not die until 1616, when he was fifty-two, he probably wrote the last play that was wholly his own work (rather than a part-work, such as *Henry VIII*) five years earlier. This final play, *The Tempest*, seems a true epilogue to that busy, twenty-year career – a coda, hinting at themes he had used before, and resolving them into a pure and serene work of the imagination. Almost as an epilogue to an epilogue, there is that speech in which Prospero, the all-powerful magician, renounces his magic and gives up his art. To many people, it has seemed an image of Shakespeare himself, making his own farewell to his craft and to his own magic:

from The Tempest

Prospero. Ye elves of hills, brooks, standing lakes, and
groves;
And ye, that on the sands with printless foot
Do chase the ebbing Neptune and do fly him
When he comes back; you demi-puppets, that
By moonshine do the green sour ringlets make
Whereof the ewe not bites; and you, whose pastime
Is to make midnight mushrooms; that rejoice
To hear the solemn curfew; by whose aid, –
Weak masters though ye be – I have bedimm'd
The noontide sun, call'd forth the mutinous winds,
And 'twixt the green sea and the azur'd vault
Set roaring war: to the dread-rattling thunder
Have I given fire and rifted Jove's stout oak
With his own bolt: the strong-bas'd promontory
Have I made shake; and by the spurs pluck'd up
The pine and cedar: graves at my command
Have wak'd their sleepers, op'd, and let them forth
By my so potent art. But this rough magic
I here abjure; and, when I have requir'd
Some heavenly music, – which even now I do, –
To work mine end upon their senses that
This airy charm is for, I'll break my staff,
Bury it certain fathoms in the earth,
And, deeper than did ever plummet sound,
I'll drown my book.

FOUR

Metaphysical and Devotional
1590-1670

It has been said that 'Power is the shaping principle in Donne's verse' –
the power of argument, of persuasion, the power of God, or of a king, or of
a fiercely wooing lover. John Donne himself was ambitious, audacious,
extreme. Later in his life he made, or tried to make, a firm distinction
between the young 'Jack Donne' (the writer of lascivious verse and
scurrilous satires) and the mature and devout 'Dr Donne' (Dean of St
Paul's, and one of the great intellectual preachers). But Jack Donne and
Dr Donne are the same man: dramatic, immediate, playing in a
deliberately exaggerated way with ideas and concepts, manipulating all

26. (right) The
ambitious young Jack
Donne aged about 23,
painted by an
unknown artist c. 1595.

27. (left) The mature
and devout Dr Donne,
Dean of St Paul's,
painted by Isaac Oliver
in 1616.

the shock tactics of his rhetoric to persuade his audience with ingenuities. In his early poem 'The Flea', for example, he argues his way through with the outrageous logic of a brilliant lawyer, hot-blooded and cold-blooded at the same time:

The Flea

Marke but this flea, and marke in this,
How little that which thou deny'st me is;
It suck'd me first, and now sucks thee,
And in this flea, our two bloods mingled bee;
Tou know'st that this cannot be said
A sinne, nor shame, nor losse of maidenhead,
Yet this enjoyes before it wooe,
And pamper'd swells with one blood made of two,
And this, alas, is more than wee would doe.

Oh stay, three lives in one flea spare,
Where wee almost, yea more than maryed are.
This flea is you and I, and this
Our mariage bed, and mariage temple is;
Though parents grudge, and you, w'are met,
And cloysterd in these living walls of jet.
Though use make you apt to kill mee,
Let not to that, selfe murder added bee,
And sacrilege, three sinnes in killing three.

Cruell and sodaine, hast thou since
Purpled thy naile, in blood of innocence?
Wherein could this flea guilty bee,
Except in that drop which it suckt from thee?
Yet thou triumph'st, and saist that thou
Find'st not thy selfe, nor mee the weaker now;
'Tis true, then learne how false feares bee;
Just so much honor, when thou yeeld'st to mee,
Will waste, as this flea's death tooke life from thee.

'The Flea' was probably written in the late sixteenth century, when Donne was in his twenties. It was a time of imperial expansion and foreign adventure, of political intrigue, and of ruthless suppression of Catholicism. Donne had been born into a Catholic family, and had relatives and friends who had been gaoled and executed for their faith. Making his ambitious way in the world, he renounced Catholicism, went on military expeditions against Spain, and was a known and witty man-about-town.

Donne's originality does not lie in his ideas, or even in his subject-matter, but in his manner of attack. The idea of a flea having commerce, as it were, between lovers, was not an entirely original one – there are other contemporary poems on the subject – but no one made such an extraordinary performance of it as Donne. The way it opens is very characteristic of him: 'Mark but this flea . . .' – a direct, almost buttonholing tone of voice, putting the reader or listener unwaveringly at the receiving end of a peremptory instruction. 'Listen, attend,' the voice says. Or it vaults right into the middle of a situation with a presumed argument: 'I wonder . . .,' he says:

The Good-Morrow

I wonder, by my troth, what thou and I
Did, till we loved? were we not weaned till then?
But sucked on country pleasures, childishly?
Or snorted we in the Seven Sleepers' den?
'Twas so; but this, all pleasures fancies be;
If ever any beauty I did see,
Which I desired, and got, 'twas but a dream of thee.

And now good-morrow to our waking souls,
Which watch not one another out of fear;
For love all love of other sights controls,
And makes one little room an everywhere.
Let sea-discoverers to new worlds have gone;
Let maps to others worlds on worlds have shown;
Let us possess one world; each hath one, and is one.

My face in thine eye, thine in mine appears,
And true plain hearts do in the faces rest;
Where can we find two better hemispheres
Without sharp north, without declining west?
Whatever dies, was not mixed equally;
If our two loves be one, or thou and I
Love so alike that none can slacken, none can die.

Donne's images and metaphors draw on every kind of fact and experience – astronomy, exploration, mythology, metalworking . . . A century and a half later, Dr Johnson was to call such almost excessive ingenuity 'metaphysical', thus giving a label to Donne and his followers that has lasted ever since. Everything is put to rhetorical use – even the sun in the sky, if need be, as in his poem 'The Sun Rising', in which what is addressed is not the loved one but the sun itself. Again, the broad theme was not an entirely original one: there are all those Provençal *aubades* (poems of dawn, when lovers must part), and medieval and renaissance English poems of the type. But there had been nothing like Donne's rapidity and vigour, that wonderfully insolent peremptoriness:

The Sun Rising

28. Donne's images and metaphors are drawn from a wide range of areas including astronomy. This sixteenth-century French picture shows an arbalest, an instrument for measuring altitudes of the stars.

Busy old fool, unruly Sun,
Why dost thou thus,
Through windows, and through curtains, call on us?
Must to thy motions lovers' seasons run?
Saucy pedantic wretch, go chide
Late school-boys and sour prentices,
Go tell court-huntsmen that the king will ride,
Call country ants to harvest offices;
Love, all alike, no season knows nor clime,
Nor hours, days, months, which are the rags of time.

Thy beams so reverend and strong
Why should'st thou think?
I could eclipse and cloud them with a wink,
But that I would not lose her sight so long.
If her eyes have not blinded thine,
Look, and to-morrow late tell me,
Whether both th'Indias of spice and mine
Be where thou left'st them, or lie here with me.
Ask for those kings whom thou saw'st yesterday,
And thou shalt hear, 'All here in one bed lay.'

She's all states, and all princes I:
Nothing else is;
Princes do but play us; compared to this,
All honour's mimic, all wealth alchemy.
Thou, Sun, art half as happy as are we,
In that the world's contracted thus;
Thine age asks ease, and since thy duties be
To warm the world, that's done by warming us.
Shine here to us, and thou art everywhere;
This bed thy centre is, these walls thy sphere.

Donne was a dramatist, though he wrote no plays. It is sometimes forgotten that Donne was just as much an Elizabethan as Shakespeare: Shakespeare's *Romeo and Juliet* and *Richard II* are probably almost exactly contemporary with many of these love poems of Donne's. This was of course the greatest age of English drama; and in such a poem as 'The Apparition' Donne creates a drama in miniature, an imagined part-playful, part-terrifying address to a young woman who has refused him:

The Apparition

When by thy scorn, O murd'ress, I am dead,
And that thou thinkst thee free
From all solicitation from me,
Then shall my ghost come to thy bed,
And thee, fain'd vestal, in worse arms shall see;
Then thy sick taper will begin to wink,
And he, whose thou art then, being tired before,
Will, if thou stir, or pinch to wake him, think
     Thou call'st for more,
And in false sleep will from thee shrink,
And then poor aspen wretch, neglected thou
Bath'd in a cold quicksilver sweat wilt lie
     A verier ghost than I;
What I will say I will not tell thee now,
Lest that preserve thee; and since my love is spent,
I had rather thou shouldst painfully repent,
Than by my threat'nings rest still innocent.

That sense of the dramatic carries over into Donne's religious poems, the best known of which are the nineteen commonly called the Holy Sonnets. When they were written is not precisely known: it has been argued that many of them may well have been written before his late ordination at the age of forty-two. They share the forceful voice of Donne's love poems, in such striking opening lines as

> At the round earth's imagined corners, blow
> Your trumpets, angels, and arise, arise
> From death, you numberless infinities

or

> Batter my heart, three-personed God

or

> What if this present were the world's last night?

Such lines have the abrupt, superbly commanding note, now directed elsewhere, of 'Busy old fool, unruly sun . . .'. And there is this elaborately disdainful address to Death, which is more like a knock-down argument than a piece of convincing reasoning:

Death, Be Not Proud

> Death, be not proud, though some have callèd thee
> Mighty and dreadful, for thou art not so:
> For those whom thou think'st thou dost overthrow
> Die not, poor Death; nor yet canst thou kill me.
> From Rest and Sleep, which but thy pictures be,
> Much pleasure, then from thee much more must flow;
> And soonest our best men with thee do go –
> Rest of their bones and souls' delivery.
> Thou'rt slave to fate, chance, kings, and desperate men,
> And dost with poison, war, and sickness dwell;
> And poppy or charms can make us sleep as well
> And better than thy stroke. Why swell'st thou then?
> One short sleep past, we wake eternally,
> And Death shall be no more: Death, thou shalt die.

Even in the extremity of illness, with his mind – as so often – set on death and punishment, Donne worked with his habitual ingenuity. Seven or eight years before his own death, while seriously ill, he could still play on the sound of his own name (*Donne, done*) and on the similar chime between the *sun* in the sky and *Thy Son*, God's son, in 'A Hymn to God the Father':

29. 'Death, be not proud . . .'. Before he died Donne posed in his shroud for a drawing, now lost. This engraving from *Death's Duell*, 1632, and the monument by Nicholas Stone in St Paul's Cathedral record Donne in a bizarre and memorable way.

A Hymn to God the Father

Wilt Thou forgive that sin where I begun,
Which is my sin though it were done before?
Wilt Thou forgive that sin through which I run
And do run still, though still I do deplore?
When Thou hast done, Thou hast not done,
For I have more.

Wilt Thou forgive that sin by which I have won
Others to sin? and made my sin their door?
Wilt Thou forgive that sin which I did shun
A year or two, but wallowed in a score?
When Thou hast done, Thou hast not done,
For I have more.

I have a sin of fear, that when I have spun
My last thread I shall perish on the shore;
Swear by Thyself that at my death Thy son
Shall shine as He shines now and heretofore;
And having done that, Thou hast done,
I fear no more.

One of John Donne's patrons and admirers was an aristocratic lady called Magdalen Herbert. It is likely that Donne gave her manuscript copies of some of his poems (they were not published until after his death in 1631), and if so they were almost certainly read by one of Magdalen Herbert's sons, George. Coming from a noble family, brought up to value

30. George Herbert, who renounced his worldly ambitions to become a country parson.

intellectual attainments, apt and practised in linguistic nimbleness, George Herbert was for much of his life ambitious for worldly success; and it seemed within reach, as he became Public Orator at Cambridge and man-about-court. But Herbert arrived at a point in his thirties when he realised that these ambitions were likely to come to nothing; and it was then that he took the unusual step, for a man of such background and attainments, of becoming a country parson, rector of a parish near Salisbury in Wiltshire. He spent his final years here at Bemerton in the happy self-abnegation of looking after his parishioners, not with resigned or bitter austerity but apparently with joy.

None of Herbert's mature poems, written in the last few years of his quite short life (he died at the age of thirty-nine) has other than a religious subject. But they are poems of great variety, both in form and in spirit. There are poems of self-doubt and self-disgust, of celebration and exaltation, and poems of a playful ingenuity. Throughout, there is a plainness, a sincerity and a homeliness that gives the impression of a domesticated John Donne: as in the way Herbert tells a story about encountering Christ in his sonnet 'Redemption':

Redemption

Having been tenant long to a rich Lord,
Not thriving, I resolvèd to be bold,
And make a suit unto Him, to afford
A new small-rented lease, and cancell th' old.

In heaven at His manour I Him sought:
They told me there, that He was lately gone
About some land, which he had deerly bought
Long since on Earth, to take possession.

I straight return'd, and knowing His great birth,
Sought Him accordingly in great resorts –
In cities, theatres, gardens, parks and courts:
At length I heard a raggèd noise and mirth
Of theeves and murderers; there I Him espied,
Who straight, 'Your suit is granted' said, and died.

But there must have been a sense of strain at times in Herbert's choice of a religious vocation; and it is that strain, that sense of rebelliousness against discipline, which he handles so dramatically, and with such an inevitable rhythm of movement towards peace, in his poem 'The Collar'. It begins with all the passion and abrupt power of Donne:

The Collar

I struck the board, and cry'd, No more;
I will abroad.
What, shall I ever sigh and pine?
My lines and life are free; free as the road,
Loose as the winde, as large as store.
Shall I be still in suit?
Have I no harvest but a thorn
To let me bloud, and not restore
What I have lost with cordiall fruit?
Sure there was wine
Before my sighs did drie it; there was corn
Before my tears did drown it;
Is the year onely lost to me?
Have I no bayes to crown it,
No flowers, no garlands gay? all blasted,
All wasted?
Not so, my heart; but there is fruit,
And thou hast hands.
Recover all thy sigh-blown age
On double pleasures; leave thy cold dispute
Of what is fit and not, forsake thy cage,
Thy rope of sands
Which pettie thoughts have made, and made to thee
Good cable, to enforce and draw,
And be thy law,
While thou didst wink and wouldst not see.
Away! take heed;
I will abroad.
Call in thy death's-head there, tie up thy fears;
He that forebears
To suit and serve his need
Deserves his load.
But as I rav'd and grew more fierce and wilde
At every word,
Methought I heard one calling, 'Childe';
And I reply'd, 'My Lord.'

That dramatic simplicity of Herbert, in which plain domestic strength and plain story-telling are compressed into something full of rhythmical subtlety and delicacy, is the note of what is probably his best-known poem, an anecdote and a dialogue called 'Love':

31. One of the Cavalier Poets,
Sir John Suckling,
painted by Anthony van Dyck.

Love

Love bade me welcome; yet my soul drew back,
Guilty of dust and sin.
But quick-eyed Love, observing me grow slack
From my first entrance in,
Drew nearer to me, sweetly questioning
If I lack'd anything.

'A guest,' I answer'd, 'worthy to be here:'
Love said, 'You shall be he.'
'I, the unkind, ungrateful? Ah, my dear,
I cannot look on Thee.'
Love took my hand and smiling did reply,
'Who made the eyes but I?'

'Truth, Lord; but I have marr'd them: let my shame
Go where it doth deserve.'
'And know you not,' says Love, 'Who bore the blame?'
'My dear, then I will serve.'
'You must sit down,' says Love, 'and taste my meat.'
So I did sit and eat.

Herbert's poems were written, and he died, not long before the English Civil War. Through that conflict, in the years leading up to it and in the aftermath of Oliver Cromwell's virtual dictatorship, poets took sides like anyone else. Among the followers of Charles I (those who have sometimes been called the Cavalier Poets) were Richard Lovelace and John Suckling. The work of both is smooth, witty, formal, and chiefly concerned with elegant and dandified variations on simple love themes. Suckling sometimes sounds like a slighter but equally cynical Donne:

Out Upon It!

Out upon it! I have lov'd
  Three whole days together;
And am like to love three more,
  If it prove fair weather.

Time shall moult away his wings,
  Ere he shall discover
In the whole wide world again
  Such a constant lover.

32. (right) Richard
Lovelace, another
Cavalier Poet, was a
professional soldier.

33. (below) This print
from *Anglia Rediviva*
by Joshua Sprigg
(1647) shows the
Royalist army facing
the New Model army,
commanded by Sir
Thomas Fairfax,
before the Battle of
Naseby, the decisive
battle of the Civil War.

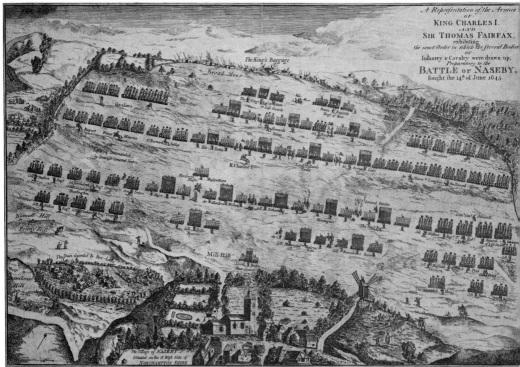

But the spite on 't is, no praise
  Is due at all to me:
Love with me had made no stays,
  Had it any been but she.

Had it any been but she,
  And that very face,
There had been at least ere this
  A dozen dozen in her place.

Lovelace is more serious, more elaborate, and his most famous poem is one that directly confronts a choice that must have been a reality, for he was a professional soldier – 'To Lucasta, Going to the Wars':

To Lucasta, Going to the Wars

Tell me not, sweet, I am unkind,
  That from the nunnery
Of thy chaste breast and quiet mind,
  To war and arms I fly.

True, a new mistress now I chase,
  The first foe in the field;
And with a stronger faith embrace
  A sword, a horse, a shield.

Yet this inconstancy is such
  As you too shall adore;
I could not love thee, dear, so much,
  Lov'd I not Honour more.

The case of Robert Herrick, though he is sometimes grouped with the Cavalier Poets, is rather different. Herrick was not part of the landed gentry, like Suckling and Lovelace. After being apprenticed to his uncle, who was a goldsmith, he went to Cambridge as a student in his early twenties, much older than was usual at the time, was ordained, and eventually in his late thirties was given a living in a remote Devon parish on the edge of Dartmoor. There he stayed (except for a period when he was ejected by the Puritans) until his death as an old man.

Though a clergyman–poet, Herrick bears no resemblance whatsoever to Herbert. All his best poems are secular, and many of them are charming flirtations with eroticism, the wistful lyrics of a bachelor who

34. Robert Herrick, a country clergyman, wrote poems celebrating love, youth and rural rites.

knows, perhaps, what he wants, but who also knows he is unlikely to get it. Beyond that, he has a strong sense of the passing of time, of *carpe diem* – that is, to catch the moment before it vanishes; as in 'To the Virgins, to make much of Time':

To the Virgins, to make much of Time

Gather ye Rose-buds while ye may,
   Old Time is still a flying:
And this same flower that smiles to day,
   To morrow will be dying.

The glorious Lamp of Heaven, the Sun,
   The higher he's a getting;
The sooner will his Race be run,
   And neerer he's to Setting.

That Age is best, which is the first,
   When Youth and Blood are warmer;
But being spent, the worse, and worst
   Times, still succeed the former.

Then be not coy, but use your time;
And while ye may, goe marry:
For having lost but once your prime,
You may for ever tarry.

But the qualities that characterise Suckling, Lovelace and Herrick are not to be found just on one side in the division between Royalists and Parliamentarians. Andrew Marvell became a consistent opponent of the King, and he sat as Member of Parliament for Hull in one of Cromwell's

35. Andrew Marvell, though a staunch Parliamentarian, was as elegant and witty as the Cavalier Poets.

last parliaments. He also, earlier on, worked as a civil servant, taking part in foreign negotiations and helping deal with foreign documents. In all this – and in his poetry – he had a sense of balance and fairness. In his lines addressed to Cromwell, in the 'Horatian Ode upon Cromwell's Return from Ireland', there is a real sympathy with the dignity of King Charles as he went to execution:

36. The execution
of Charles I.

He nothing common did or mean
Upon that memorable scene;
But with his keener eye
The Axe's edge did try:

Nor called the Gods with vulgar spite
To vindicate his helpless right,
But bowed his comely head
Down, as upon a bed.

Along with Marvell's balance and fairness goes his elegance: he was as smooth and witty and formal as the Cavalier poets – most persuasively in one of his love poems, a beautiful piece of argumentativeness of which Donne would have approved: 'To his Coy Mistress':

To his Coy Mistress

Had we but world enough, and time,
This coyness, lady, were no crime.
We would sit down, and think which way
To walk, and pass our long love's day.
Thou by the Indian Ganges' side
Should'st rubies find: I by the tide
Of Humber would complain. I would
Love you ten years before the Flood,
And you should, if you please, refuse
Till the conversion of the Jews.
My vegetable love should grow
Vaster than empires, and more slow.
An hundred years should go to praise
Thine eyes, and on thy forehead gaze:
Two hundred to adore each breast;
But thirty thousand to the rest;
An age at least to every part,
And the last age should show your heart.
For, lady, you deserve this state,
Nor would I love at lower rate.
   But at my back I always hear
Time's wingèd chariot hurrying near:
And yonder all before us lie
Deserts of vast eternity.
Thy beauty shall no more be found;
Nor, in thy marble vault, shall sound
My echoing song: then worms shall try
That long-preserved virginity,
And your quaint honour turn to dust,
And into ashes all my lust.
The grave's a fine and private place,
But none, I think, do there embrace.
   Now, therefore, while the youthful hue
Sits on thy skin like morning dew,
And while thy willing soul transpires

At every pore with instant fires,
Now let us sport us while we may;
And now, like amorous birds of prey,
Rather at once our Time devour,
Than languish in his slow-chapt power.
Let us roll all our strength and all
Our sweetness up into one ball,
And tear our pleasures with rough strife
Thorough the iron gates of life.
Thus, though we cannot make our Sun
Stand still, yet we will make him run.

As a civil servant, Andrew Marvell was for a time the chief assistant in the Latin Secretaryship, translating and framing diplomatic documents, to the greatest poet of the age in this mid seventeenth century: John Milton. Milton was more clearly a Puritan, more ambitiously and prolifically a poet, than Marvell; and the next section is wholly given over to him, and particularly to Milton's masterpiece, the one undoubted epic poem in English – *Paradise Lost*.

FIVE

Milton
1608 - 74

The opening lines of John Milton's *Paradise Lost*, which we shall come to in a moment, set out the long-pondered argument of a poet who by the time he wrote them was, one might say, in voluntary internal exile. Milton by now was in his fifties, stripped of all the political responsibilities he had held during Cromwell's rule, stripped of most of his property, fined, protected from worse revenges by the efforts of a few loyal friends. He was also by now totally blind, able to compose only in his head and to dictate his words to an amanuensis.

This was the man who, as an undergraduate at Christ's College, Cambridge, in the 1620s had been so beautiful that he was known as 'the Lady' of his college; who, supported by his father's belief in him, studied and travelled on his own for years, preparing for the great work he knew he had it in him to write; but who in 1660, at the Restoration of Charles II, saw behind him the wreck of his life as a valued councillor of the State, the deaths of two wives, and – as for his writing – mainly the reputation of being a dangerously radical pamphleteer.

But Milton knew he was great. He knew it was a matter of time, study and perseverance. While he was still young, he wrote to a friend:

> You ask me what I am thinking of? So may the good Deity help me, – of Immortality! And what am I doing? *Growing my wings.*

If such answers sound inhuman, well, there *was* something uncommonly proud, withdrawn and dedicated about Milton. The estrangement of his first wife probably resulted from this principled aloofness. But if proof were needed that he could have profoundly human feelings of love and loss, there is the sonnet he wrote in 1658 after the death of his second wife, Katherine. She had never recovered from giving birth to a child (who died six weeks later). Milton had already been blind for several years when he married Katherine; he never saw her – 'her face was vail'd', as he says in the poem, 'On His Deceased Wife'. He would see her in heaven . . . :

37. John Milton,
the 'Lady' of Christ's College,
by an unknown artist
c. 1629.

On His Deceased Wife

Methought I saw my late espousèd Saint
Brought to me like Alcestis from the grave,
Whom Joves great Son to her glad Husband gave,
Rescu'd from death by force though pale and faint,
Mine as whom washt from spot of child-bed taint,
Purification in the old Law did save,
And such, as yet once more I trust to have
Full sight of her in Heaven without restraint,
Came vested all in white, pure as her mind:
Her face was vail'd, yet to my fancied sight,
Love, sweetness, goodness, in her person shin'd
So clear, as in no face with more delight.
But O as to embrace me she enclin'd
I wak'd, she fled, and day brought back my night.

For many years Milton had the ambition to write an epic. First it was to be an Arthurian epic. But after he came back from his travels in Italy in his early thirties, he wrote down a list of almost a hundred subjects for a large-scale work, and increasingly over the years his mind turned towards a drama or epic on Adam and Eve. As he saw it, such a work would need to treat the incidents that led up to their Creation and their Fall – to see them foreshadowed in the Fall of Satan himself; and to do that it had to go back to the original Chaos, the 'vast Abyss' over which God brooded and out of which he created everything. So, quite consciously in the spirit of Homer and Virgil in their own ancient epics, Milton begins with an invocation to the Heavenly Muse, an invocation which is also in some sense a synopsis of all that will follow: War in Heaven, the Fall of Man, an attempt to 'justify' (that is, vindicate) 'the ways of God to men':

from Paradise Lost, Book I

Of Mans first disobedience, and the Fruit
Of that Forbidden Tree, whose mortal tast
Brought death into the world, and all our woe,
With loss of Eden, till one greater Man
Restore us, and regain the blissful seat,
Sing Heav'nly Muse, that on the secret top
Of Oreb, or of Sinai, didst inspire
That shepherd, who first taught the chosen seed,
In the beginning how the Heav'ns and earth
Rose out of Chaos: Or if Sion Hill

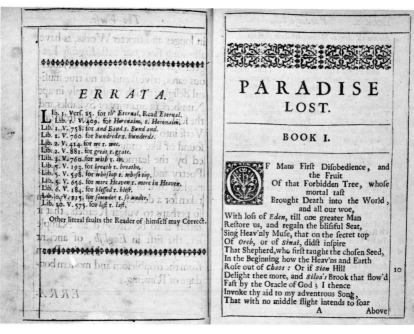

38. An early edition of *Paradise Lost* (1669).

Delight thee more, and Siloa's brook that flow'd
East by the oracle of God; I thence
Invoke thy aid to my adventrous song,
That with no middle flight intends to soar
Above th'Aonian mount, while it pursues
Things unattempted yet in Prose or Rhime.
And chiefly Thou O Spirit, that dost prefer
Before all temples th'upright heart and pure,
Instruct me, for Thou know'st; Thou from the first
Wast present, and with mighty wings outspread
Dove-like satst brooding on the vast Abyss
And mad'st it pregnant: what in me is dark
Illumine, what is low raise and support;
That to the highth of this great Argument
I may assert Eternal Providence,
And justifie the wayes of God to men.

'Things unattempted yet in Prose or Rhyme': there at the beginning we have quite explicitly the exalted ambition Milton set himself. And what things! A cast-list of God, Satan, good angels, bad angels, Sin, Death, titanic struggles, cosmic villains. . . . For this stupendous adventure Milton felt that the necessary technical instrument could not be what he called 'the jingling sound of like endings' (that is, rhyme), but the English equivalent of the unrhymed achievements of Homer in Greek and Virgil in Latin. Milton himself called it 'English heroic verse without rhyme'. In some ways, it is a very grand and learned development of Shakespeare's noblest blank verse in his tragedies; but it is far more complex in its long serpentine sentences, its expressive and endlessly varying rhythms.

The first great speech of the poem is in Book I of the twelve books. Satan, cast down by God to Hell with the other rebel angels, sees close by him 'One next himself in power and next in crime' – Beelzebub, Satan's lieutenant. Satan addresses Beelzebub like this:

39. Satan and the Rebel Angels by William Blake, from Book I of *Paradise Lost.*

from Paradise Lost, Book I

If thou beest he; but O how fall'n! how chang'd
From him, who in the happy Realms of Light
Cloth'd with transcendent brightness didst out-shine
Myriads though bright: If he whom mutual league,
United thoughts and counsels, equal hope
And hazard in the Glorious Enterprize,
Joynd with me once, now misery hath joynd
In equal ruin: into what Pit thou seest
From what highth fall'n, so much the stronger prov'd
He with his Thunder: and till then who knew
The force of those dire Arms? yet not for those
Nor what the Potent Victor in his rage
Can else inflict do I repent or change,
Though chang'd in outward lustre; that fixt mind
And high disdain, from sence of injur'd merit,
That with the mightiest rais'd me to contend,
And to the fierce contention brought along
Innumerable force of Spirits arm'd
That durst dislike his reign, and me preferring,
His utmost power with adverse power oppos'd
In dubious Battel on the Plains of Heav'n,
And shook his throne. What though the field be lost?
All is not lost; the unconquerable Will,
And study of revenge, immortal hate,
And courage never to submit or yield:
And what is else not to be overcome?
That Glory never shall his wrath or might
Extort from me. To bow and sue for grace
With suppliant knee, and deifie his power
Who from the terrour of this Arm so late
Doubted his Empire, that were low indeed,
That were an ignominy and shame beneath
This downfall; since by Fate the strength of Gods
And this Empyreal substance cannot fail,
Since through experience of this great event
In Arms not worse, in foresight much advanc't,
We may with more successful hope resolve
To wage by force or guile eternal Warr
Irreconcileable, to our grand Foe,
Who now triumphs, and in th'excess of joy
Sole reigning holdst the Tyranny of Heav'n.

It sounds, as it is intended to do, like the high-pitched speech of a military warlord, a generalissimo. God is the poem's hero and Satan's enemy; but it is often Satan who is given the most marvellously rhetorical lines.

But the real voice of *Paradise Lost*, whichever character is actually speaking, is Milton's: a subtle, flexible, complex, grand and resonant voice, full of rich allusions, exotic place-names, and in complete control of the hovering, circling, weaving and weighty syntax. Very occasionally, one can hear Milton speaking in his own person, not just as narrator or dramatiser but directly from his own heart; for example, briefly at the beginning of Book VII, out of his powerless isolation in 1660 and after:

> though fall'n on evil days,
> On evil days though fall'n, and evil tongues;
> In darkness, and with dangers compassed round,
> And solitude . . .

40. A bust of Milton, c. 1660, after he became blind.

Most poignantly and powerfully, there is the opening of Book III, when he speaks out of his blindness in a great hymn to Light:

from Paradise Lost, Book III

Hail holy light, offspring of Heav'n first-born,
Or of th'Eternal Coeternal beam
May I express thee unblam'd? since God is light,
And never but in unapproachèd light
Dwelt from Eternitie, dwelt then in thee,
Bright effluence of bright essence increate.
Or hear'st thou rather pure Ethereal stream,
Whose fountain who shall tell? before the Sun,
Before the Heavens thou wert, and at the voice
Of God, as with a Mantle didst invest
The rising world of waters dark and deep,
Won from the void and formless infinite.
Thee I re-visit now with bolder wing,
Escap't the Stygian pool, though long detain'd
In that obscure sojourn, while in my flight
Through utter and through middle darkness borne
With other notes then to th'Orphean Lyre
I sung of Chaos and Eternal Night,
Taught by the heaven'ly Muse to venture down
The dark descent, and up to reascend,
Though hard and rare: thee I revisit safe,
And feel thy sovran vital Lamp; but thou
Revisit'st not these eyes, that rowle in vain
To find thy piercing ray, and find no dawn;
So thick a drop serene hath quenched thir Orbs,
Or dim suffusion veild. Yet not the more
Cease I to wander where the Muses haunt
Cleer Spring, or shadie Grove, or Sunnie Hill,
Smit with the love of sacred song; but chief
Thee Sion and the flowrie Brooks beneath
That wash thy hallowd feet, and warbling flow,
Nightly I visit: nor somtimes forget
Those other two equal'd with me in Fate,
So were I equal'd with them in renown,
Blind Thamyris and blind Maeonides,
And Tiresias and Phineus Prophets old.
Then feed on thoughts, that voluntarie move
Harmonious numbers; as the wakeful Bird
Sings darkling, and in shadiest Covert hid
Tunes her nocturnal Note. Thus with the Year
Seasons return, but not to me returns

Day, or the sweet approach of Ev'n or Morn
Or sight of vernal bloom, or Summers Rose,
Or flocks, or herds, or human face divine;
But cloud instead, and ever-during dark
Surrounds me, from the chearful waies of men
Cut off, and for the Book of knowledge fair
Presented with a Universal blanc
Of Natures works to mee expung'd and ras'd,
And wisdome at one entrance quite shut out.
So much the rather thou Celestial light
Shine inward, and the mind through all her powers
Irradiate, there plant eyes, all mist from thence
Purge and disperse, that I may see and tell
Of things invisible to mortal sight.

Much of *Paradise Lost* is cast in the form of a great debate, of arguments
and counter-arguments between such protagonists as Satan and the
Angel Gabriel. Interleaved with the debates are passages which seem as if
spoken by some sublime commentator who stands above these planetary
exchanges and orders of cosmic battle. The voice of this commentator is

41. An illustration
from *Paradise Lost*
showing Adam and
Eve surmounted by
Milton.

of course Milton's; but it is his voice in its guise of epic narrator, the vigorous, almost god-like, self-appointed heir of Homer in the *Iliad* or Virgil in the *Aeneid*, or perhaps most closely the Dante of *The Divine Comedy*. We hear that voice at the end of Book IV, following the description of Satan surrounded by his angels, threatened by Gabriel and the others, during the War in Heaven:

from Paradise Lost, Book IV

While thus he spake, th'Angelic Squadron bright
Turnd fierie red, sharpning in moonèd hornes
Thir Phalanx, and began to hemm him round
With ported Spears, as thick as when a field
Of Ceres ripe for harvest waving bends
Her bearded Grove of ears, which way the wind
Swayes them; the careful Plowman doubting stands
Least on the threshing floore his hopeful sheaves
Prove chaff. On th'other side Satan allarm'd
Collecting all his might dilated stood,
Like Teneriff or Atlas unremov'd:
His stature reacht the Skie, and on his Crest
Sat horror Plum'd; nor wanted in his graspe
What seemed both Spear and Shield: now dreadful
    deeds
Might have ensu'd, nor onely Paradise
In this commotion, but the Starrie Cope
Of Heav'n perhaps, or all the Elements
At least had gon to rack, disturbd and torne
With violence of this conflict, had not soon
Th'Eternal to prevent such horrid fray
Hung forth in Heav'n his golden Scales, yet seen
Betwixt Astrea and the Scorpion signe,
Wherein all things created first he weighd,
The pendulous round Earth with ballanc't Aire
In counterpoise, now ponders all events,
Battels and Realms: In these he put two weights
The sequel each of parting and of fight;
The latter quick up flew, and kickt the beam.

So Satan, hindered (as Milton puts it in the prose 'Argument' he attached to the poem) 'by a sign from Heaven, flies out of Paradise'. From then on, in spite of Raphael's explanations to Adam and Eve of what these battles mean, the reasons for and manner of the Creation, the dangers

42. Eve accepts the forbidden fruit from Adam.

attendant on the two innocents, it is only a matter of time for Satan to return 'with meditated guile' in the form of the Serpent, and for the whole predestined story to work itself out. Eve eats the forbidden fruit; Adam follows her example; the guardian angels forsake Paradise; the Son of God intercedes for 'our first parents'. But the decree is that they must be banished from the Garden. So, at the conclusion of the final book of *Paradise Lost*, Book XII, the Angel Michael leads Adam and Eve out of Paradise. They are reconciled, chastened; there is hope, in the distance. Michael speaks at the beginning:

from Paradise Lost, Book XII

This having learnt, thou hast attaind the summe
Of wisdome; hope no higher, though all the Starrs
Thou knewst by name, and all th'ethereal Powers,
All secrets of the deep, all natures works,
Or works of God in Heav'n, Air, Earth, or Sea,
And all the riches of this World enjoydst,
And all the rule, one Empire; only add

Deeds to thy knowledge answerable, add Faith,
Add Vertue, Patience, Temperance, add Love,
By name to come call'd charitie, the soul
Of all the rest: then wilt thou not be loath
To leave this Paradise, but shalt possess
A Paradise within thee, happier farr.
Let us descend now therefore from this top
Of Speculation; for the hour precise
Exacts our parting hence; and see the guards,
By mee encampt on yonder Hill, expect
Thir motion, at whose front a flaming Sword,
In signal of remove, waves fiercely round;
We may no longer stay: go, waken Eve;
Her also I with gentle dreams have calm'd
Portending good, and all her spirits compos'd
To meek submission: thou at season fit
Let her with thee partake what thou hast heard,
Chiefly what may concern her Faith to know,
The great deliverance by her Seed to come
(For by the Womans Seed) on all Mankind.
That ye may live, which will be many dayes,
Both in one Faith unanimous though sad,
With cause for evils past, yet much more cheer'd
With meditation on the happie end.
    He ended, and they both descend the Hill;
Descended, Adam to the Bowre where Eve
Lay sleeping ran before, but found her wak't;
And thus with words not sad she him receav'd.
    Whence thou returnst, and whither wentst, I know;
For God is also in sleep, and dreams advise,
Which he hath sent propitious, some great good
Presaging, since with sorrow and hearts distress
Wearied I fell asleep: but now lead on;
In mee is no delay; with thee to goe,
Is to stay here; without thee here to stay,
Is to go hence unwilling; thou to mee
Art all things under Heav'n, all places thou,
Who for my wilful crime art banisht hence.
This further consolation yet secure
I carry hence; though all by mee is lost,
Such favour I unworthie am voutsaft,
By mee the Promis'd Seed shall all restore.
    So spake our Mother Eve, and Adam heard
Well pleas'd, but answer'd not; for now too nigh

Th'Archangel stood, and from the other Hill
To thir fixt station, all in bright array
The Cherubim descended: on the ground
Gliding meteorous, as Ev'ning Mist
Ris'n from a River o're the marish glides,
And gathers ground fast at the Labourers heel
Homeward returning. High in Front advanc't,
The brandisht Sword of God before them blaz'd
Fierce as a comet; which with torrid heat,
And vapour as the Libyan air adust,
Began to parch that temperate clime; whereat
In either hand the hastning Angel caught
Our lingring Parents, and to th'Eastern gate
Led them direct, and down the Cliff as fast
To the subjected Plaine; then disappeer'd.
They looking back, all th'Eastern side beheld
Of Paradise, so late thir happie seat,
Wav'd over by that flaming Brand, the Gate
With dreadful faces throng'd and fierie armes:
Some natural tears they drop't, but wip'd them soon;
The World was all before them, where to choose
Thir place of rest, and Providence thir guide:
They hand in hand with wandring steps and slow,
Through Eden took thir solitarie way.

So Milton ends what has been called the last classical epic, the first modern novel. In spite of Milton's withdrawal from the world, when *Paradise Lost* was first published in 1667 it was noticed quite quickly and even revered. It went into a second edition in 1674, the year of his death, and from then on it became a commercial success (though Milton himself received only £10 for it) and a potent influence on thought in general and poetry in particular. The age to come, more worldly in many ways, was nevertheless prepared to see it as a great monument. Today we are bound to have our difficulties with *Paradise Lost*; but – as one of its modern editors, Douglas Bush, has put it – if the imagination of the modern reader cannot go along with

> Milton's passionate faith in God and freewill and the attainment of a 'paradise within', he can at least hardly fail to respond to a compassionate myth of the precarious human situation, a myth which in one way or another comprehends all that mankind has felt and thought and done throughout the course of history.

43. John Wilmot,
Earl of Rochester,
courtier and highly regarded
satirical poet.

SIX

Restoration and Augustan
1660-1745

Were I, who to my cost already am
One of those strange, prodigious Creatures Man,
A spirit free to choose for my own share
What case of Flesh and Blood I'd please to wear,
I'd be a Dog, a Monkey or a Bear,
Or anything but that vain Animal
Who is so proud of being Rational.

When John Wilmot, Earl of Rochester, wrote those lines some time in the early 1670s, he was part of the cynical, selfish, rapacious high-living and low-living court of Charles II. Rochester called the poem from which the lines come 'A Satire Against Reason and Mankind'; and yet they seem, in a perverse way, to usher in what has been called the 'Age of Reason', in their scepticism rather than their disillusionment. Rochester himself was extravagant, wild, obscene, a great roisterer and drinker (he said on his deathbed that 'for five years together' he was continually drunk); and he died of his excesses at the age of thirty-three. What he left behind was not only a notorious reputation as a profligate and wit, but an almost equally high reputation as a poet: as a contemporary seventeenth-century commentator put it, 'one man reads Milton, forty Rochester'. And it was as a writer of satire that he was particularly known.

The period of eighty or so years, from the Restoration of Charles II in 1660 until the deaths of Alexander Pope and Jonathan Swift in 1744 and 1745, is the great age of satirical English poetry. It is a poetry that can be savage and elegant, specifically contemptuous and energetically grand, all at the same time. Names are named – often disguised names, but this was a tight-knit intellectual and aristocratic society in which everyone knew everyone else, and the references would not be missed. It was also a society in which misanthropy, loathing of mankind, could well seem truly founded. Rochester's 'Satire Against Reason and Mankind', part of which follows, is contemptuous and witty, loathing and self-loathing:

from A Satire Against Reason and Mankind

Were I, who to my cost already am
One of those strange, prodigious Creatures Man,
A spirit free to choose for my own share
What case of Flesh and Blood I'd please to wear,
I'd be a Dog, a Monkey or a Bear,
Or anything but that vain Animal
Who is so proud of being Rational.
The Senses are too gross, and he'll contrive
A sixth, to contradict the other five;
And before certain Instinct, will prefer
Reason, which fifty times for one does err.
Reason, an Ignis fatuus in the Mind,
Which leaves the Light of Nature (Sense) behind;
Pathless and dangerous, wandering ways it takes
Through Error's fenny Boggs and thorny Brakes;
Whilst the misguided Follower climbs with Pain
Mountains of Whimseys, heaped in his own Brain:
Stumbling from thought to thought, falls headlong down
Into Doubt's boundless Sea, where like to drown
Books bear him up a while, and make him try
To swim with Bladders of Philosophy;
In hopes still to'ertake the escaping Light
The Vapour dances in his dazzled Sight
Till spent, it leaves him to eternal night.
Then old Age and Experience hand in hand
Lead him to Death, and make him understand,
After a search so painful and so long,
That all his Life he has been in the wrong:
Huddled in Dirt this reasoning Engine lies
Who was so Proud, so Witty, and so Wise.

For all his skill, Rochester was by no means a professional poet, not even a professional writer at all. Professional writers hardly existed at the time, except in the theatre. Rochester's longer-lived contemporary, John Dryden, *was* a professional writer, and one of considerable range, who in his lifetime was as much known for his plays (by which he chiefly earned his living) as for his poems. Dryden was also very much a *public* writer: his first notable verses were an elegy on Cromwell, published when he was twenty-eight. A year later, equally public and professional, he published a

44. John Dryden is well known both for
his satirical poetry and for his plays.

poem on 'the happy restoration and return of his sacred majesty' Charles
II, and a year after that a panegyric on Charles's coronation. Dryden's
enemies didn't forget those verses on Cromwell; but he had played his
cards right, and before long he was appointed Poet Laureate.

Towards the end of his life, he wrote in a letter: 'They say my talent is satire. If it be so, 'tis a fruitful age, and there is an extraordinary crop to gather'. Some of that crop was literary, some political. Of Dryden's literary satire, 'MacFlecknoe' is his masterpiece. In 'MacFlecknoe' the main targets are two actual poets, in particular Thomas Shadwell. Dryden imagines another poet, Richard Flecknoe, lying on his deathbed and appointing Shadwell to be his true successor as monarch of 'the Realms of Nonsense'. As in almost all his satirical poetry – and as in most of the poetry in this section – the form Dryden used was the rhyming couplet, the so-called 'heroic couplet': often *mock*-heroic, in that it is deliberately inflating trivial things and third-rate people as if they were majestic participants in a noble epic. These are the opening lines of Dryden's 'MacFlecknoe':

from MacFlecknoe

All human things are subject to decay,
And, when Fate summons, Monarchs must obey:
This Fleckno found, who, like Augustus, young
Was call'd to empire, and had govern'd long:
In prose and verse, was own'd, without dispute
Through all the realms of Non-sense, absolute.
This agèd prince now flourishing in peace,
And blest with issue of a large increase,
Worn out with business, did at length debate
To settle the succession of the state:
And pond'ring which of all his sons was fit
To reign, and wage immortal war with wit;
Cry'd, 'tis resolv'd; for Nature pleads that he
Should onely rule, who most resembles me:
Shadwell alone my perfect image bears,
Mature in dullness from his tender years.
Shadwell alone, of all my sons, is he
Who stands confirm'd in full stupidity.
The rest to some faint meaning make pretence,
But Shadwell never deviates into sense.
Some beams of wit on other souls may fall,
Strike through and make a lucid interval;
But Shadwell's genuine night admits no ray,
His rising fogs prevail upon the day:
Besides his goodly fabrick fills the eye,
And seems design'd for thoughtless majesty:
Thoughtless as Monarch Oakes, that shade the plain,
And, spread in solemn state, supinely reign.

45. Charles II
appointed Dryden
his Poet Laureate.

At the same time, Dryden found more important targets among some of the members of a court faction which seemed to him dangerous to Charles II – in particular the Earl of Shaftesbury, the Duke of Buckingham and the Duke of Monmouth. Under an elaborate but transparent code of names drawn from the Bible, he used his satire as a direct political weapon. Take Charles to be King David, plotted against in the Bible; then Shaftesbury becomes Achitophel, Buckingham becomes Zimri and Monmouth becomes Absalom. The result was Dryden's long poem *Absalom and Achitophel*, a marvellous piece of public poetry. The passage that follows looks at Buckingham, in the guise of Zimri. Buckingham was himself a wit and a playwright, and he had already satirised Dryden in one of his own plays. But through its tough vigour, Dryden's portrait survives, and whatever Buckingham said is now forgotten:

from Absalom and Achitophel

Some of their chiefs were princes of the land:
In the first rank of these did Zimri stand:
A man so various, that he seem'd to be
Not one, but all Mankind's epitome.
Stiff in opinions, always in the wrong;
Was every thing by starts, and nothing long:
But, in the course of one revolving moon,
Was chymist, fidler, states-man, and buffoon:
Then all for women, painting, rhiming, drinking;
Besides ten thousand freaks that dy'd in thinking.
Blest Madman, who could every hour employ,
With something New to wish, or to enjoy!
Railing and praising were his usual theams;
And both (to shew his judgement) in extreams;
So over violent, or over civil,
That every man, with him, was God or Devil.
In squandering wealth was his peculiar art:
Nothing went unrewarded, but desert.
Begger'd by fools, whom still he found too late:
He had his jest, and they had his estate.
He laugh'd himself from court; then sought relief
By forming parties, but could ne'r be chief:
For, spight of him, the weight of business fell
On Absalom and wise Achitophel:
Thus, wicked but in will, of means bereft,
He left not Faction, but of that was left.

Jonathan Swift is best known today as the author of *Gulliver's Travels*. He began writing poems as a young man in his twenties, and it is said that Dryden greeted these early efforts with the remark, 'Cousin Swift, you will never be a poet'. Certainly Swift always thought of Dryden with malevolence. But in fact he wrote a great deal of poetry, much of it very good and most of it rather more genial and rather less savage than his prose. By this time – that is, by the early eighteenth century – there was a

46. Jonathan Swift, author of the satirical *Gulliver's Travels*, also wrote a great deal of poetry.

large number of professional writers: journalists, hacks, poetasters. Swift, though ordained a clergyman, was also a professional writer, with a haughty and sardonic view of the mob of struggling mercenary writers, the denizens of Grub Street, and those bad poets who filled the pages of the press. Using shorter rhyming lines than the 'heroic couplets' of Dryden, Swift managed something nimble, dry and astringent, as in his mocking piece 'On Poetry, a Rhapsody', from which these lines are taken:

from On Poetry, A Rhapsody

Hobbes clearly proves that ev'ry Creature
Lives in a state of War by Nature.
The Greater for the Smaller watch,
But meddle seldom with their Match.
A Whale of mod'rate Size will draw
A shole of Herrings down his Maw;
A Fox with Geese his Belly crams;
A Wolf destroys a thousand Lambs.
But, search among the rhiming Race,
The Brave are worry'd by the Base.
If, on Parnassus' Top you sit,
You rarely bite, are always bit:
Each Poet of inferior Size
On you shall rail and criticize;
And try to tear you Limb from Limb,
While others do as much for him:
The Vermin only teaze and pinch
Their Foes superior by an Inch.
So, Nat'ralists observe, a Flea
Hath smaller Fleas that on him prey,
And these have smaller yet to bite 'em,
And so proceed ad infinitum:
Thus ev'ry Poet in his Kind,
Is bit by him that comes behind;
Who, tho' too little to be seen,
Can Teaze, and gall, and give the Spleen;
Call Dunces, Fools, and Sons of Whores,
Lay Grub-Street at each others Doors:
Extol the Greek and Roman Masters,
And curse our modern Poetasters:
Complain, as many an ancient Bard did,
How Genius is no more rewarded:
How wrong a Taste prevails among us;
How much our Ancestors out-sung us;
Can personate an aukward Scorn
For those who are not Poets born:
And all their Brother Dunces lash,
Who crowd the Press with hourly Trash.

London Published by Alex^r Hogg at the King's Arms N^o16 Paternoster Row

A Prospect *of* DUBLIN*, the Capital of* Ireland

47. Dublin about the time when Swift lived there
as Dean of St Patrick's Cathedral.

Swift was Anglo-Irish: he was born in Dublin of English parents and
later became Dean of St Patrick's Cathedral in that city. Though he had
hoped for a post in England, and in some ways felt isolated in Ireland, his
attitude to the Irish people was a great deal more understanding and
liberal than that of many Englishmen before and since. It was during his
time in Ireland, and thinking of his friends there as well as in England,
that he wrote his delightful long poem 'Verses on the Death of Dr Swift',
with gaiety, with little digs at friends and enemies, and with a proper view
of his own kind of satire. Here is part of that mocking self-elegy:

from Verses on the Death of Dr Swift

> Behold the fatal Day arrive!
> How is the Dean? He's just alive.
> Now the departing Pray'r is read:
>   He hardly breathes. The Dean is dead.
> Before the Passing-Bell begun,

The News thro' half the Town has run.
O, may we all for Death prepare!
What has he left? And Who's his Heir?
I know no more than what the News is,
'Tis all bequeath'd to Publick Uses.
To Publick Use! a perfect Whim!
What had the Publick done for him!
Mere Envy, Avarice, and Pride!
He gave it all: – But, first he dy'd.
And had the Dean, in all the Nation,
No worthy Friend, no poor Relation?
So ready to do Strangers good,
Forgetting his own Flesh and Blood?

Here shift the Scene, to represent
How those I love, my Death lament,
Poor POPE will grieve a Month; and GAY
A Week; and ARBUTHNOT a Day.

St John himself will scarce forbear
To bite his Pen, and drop a Tear.
The rest will give a Shrug, and cry,
I'm sorry; but we all must dye.

My female Friends, whose tender Hearts
Have better learn'd to act their Parts,
Receive the News in doleful Dumps,
The Dean is dead (and what is Trumps?)
The Lord have Mercy on his Soul
(Ladies I'll venture for the Vole)
Six Deans they say must bear the Pall,
(I wish I knew what King to call.)
Madam, your Husband will attend
The Funeral of so good a friend.
No Madam, 'tis a shocking Sight,
And he's engag'd Tomorrow Night!
My Lady Club wou'd take it ill
If he shou'd fail her at Quadrill.
He lov'd the Dean. (I led a Heart.)
But, dearest Friends, they say, must part.
His Time was come, he ran his Race;
We hope he's in a better Place.

Perhaps I may allow, the Dean
Had too much Satyr in his Vein;
And seem'd determined not to starve it,
Because no Age could more deserve it.
Yet, Malice never was his Aim;
He lash'd the Vice, but spar'd the Name.
No Individual could resent,
Where Thousands equally were meant:
His Satyr points at no Defect,
But what all Mortals may correct;
For, he abbhor'd that senseless Tribe
Who call it Humour when they jibe:
He spar'd a Hump or crooked Nose,
Whose owners set not up for Beaux.
True genuine Dulness mov'd his Pity,
Unless it offer'd to be witty.
Those, who their Ignorance confess'd,
He ne'er offended with a Jest;
But, laugh'd to hear an Idiot quote
A Verse from Horace, learn'd by Rote.

He knew an hundred pleasant Stories,
With all the turns of Whigs and Tories:
Was chearful to his dying Day,
And Friends would let him have his Way.

He gave the little Wealth he had,
To build a House for Fools and Mad:
And shew'd by one satyric Touch,
No Nation wanted it so much;
That Kingdom he hath left his Debtor,
I wish it soon may have a Better.

One of Swift's closest friends and greatest admirers was Alexander Pope. Twenty years younger than Swift, Pope was a notable early developer – a prodigy, in fact, who was already writing well in his teens, and who wrote one of his masterpieces, 'An Essay on Criticism', when he was only twenty-one. Prevented by his lameness and general ill-health from formally attending school, and prevented by his Roman Catholic faith from attending university, he had sufficient income from his father simply to read and to write. He quickly became a financial success as a

48. (above) Charles
Jervas painted his
friend Alexander Pope
looking small, awkward
and sensitive, but
without emphasising
his physical disabilities.
The 'Muse' figure is
probably Pope's
lifelong friend Martha
Blount.

49. (below) A Hogarth
caricature of Pope
enjoying coffee-house
society.

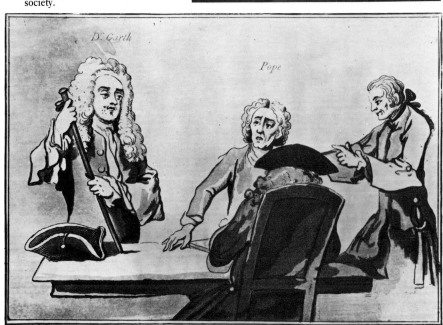

poet. By the age of thirty he was rich and famous. Looking back at his early years, he wrote:

> Why did I write? what sin to me unknown
> Dipt me in ink, my parents', or my own?
> As yet a child, nor yet a fool to fame,
> I lisp'd in numbers, for the numbers came.
> I left no calling for this idle trade,
> No duty broke, no father dis-obey'd.
> The muse but serv'd to ease some friend, not wife,
> To help me thro' this long disease, my life . . .

These lines come from a verse-letter to a friend, the 'Epistle to Dr Arbuthnot'. Someone as successful and waspish as Pope was bound to make enemies. One of these was Lord Hervey. In the 'Epistle to Dr Arbuthnot', Hervey is held up to incomparable scorn, loathing and vituperation, under the name 'Sporus':

from Epistle to Dr Arbuthnot

50. Lord Hervey,
target of Pope's
satirical 'Epistle to Dr
Arbuthnot'.

> Let Sporus tremble – *A.* What? that thing of silk,
> Sporus, that mere white curd of ass's milk?
> Satire or sense, alas! can Sporus feel?
> Who breaks a butterfly upon a wheel?
> *P.* Yet let me flap this bug with gilded wings,
> This painted child of dirt, that stinks and stings;
> Whose buzz the witty and the fair annoys,
> Yet wit ne'er tastes, and beauty ne'er enjoys:
> So well-bred spaniels civilly delight
> In mumbling of the game they dare not bite.
> Eternal smiles his emptiness betray,
> As shallow streams run dimpling all the way.
> Whether in florid impotence he speaks,
> And, as the prompter breathes, the puppet squeaks;
> Or at the ear of Eve, familiar Toad,
> Half froth, half venom, spits himself abroad,
> In puns, or politics, or tales, or lies,
> Or spite, or smut, or rhymes, or blasphemies.
> His wit all see-saw, between *that* and *this*,
> Now high, now low, now master up, now miss,
> And he himself one vile Antithesis.
> Amphibious thing! that acting either part,
> The trifling head or the corrupted heart,

Fop at the toilet, flatt'rer at the board,
Now trips a Lady, and now struts a Lord.
Eve's tempter thus the rabbins have exprest,
A cherub's face, a reptile all the rest;
Beauty that shocks you, parts that none will trust;
Wit that can creep, and pride that licks the dust.

Earlier, and in a number of different versions and revisions, Pope had
published a massive mock-heroic poem on what he saw as the powerful
and creeping diseases of pedantry, pretentiousness, commercialism and
sheer bad writing. He called it *The Dunciad*, in imitation of Homer's *Iliad*

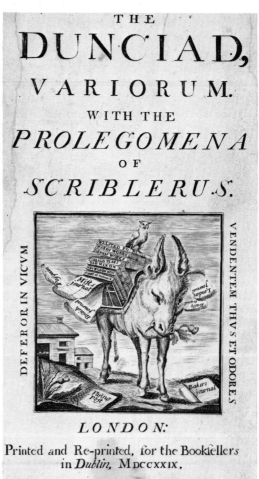

51. The title page of
Pope's mock-heroic
The Dunciad.

(the whole of which he translated into English verse) and of Virgil's
Aeneid. As a lurid vision of the triumph of Chaos and Dullness, *The
Dunciad* is like a beautifully organised nightmare. In its pessimism, it is
worthy of Swift's blackest prose – and indeed Pope dedicated it to Swift.
Here is a prophecy of the death of the Age of Reason, in its closing lines:

from The Dunciad

In vain, in vain, – the all-composing Hour
Resistless falls: The muse obeys the pow'r.
She comes! she comes! the sable Throne behold
Of night Primaeval, and of Chaos old!
Before her, Fancy's gilded clouds decay,
And all its varying Rain-bows die away.
Wit shoots in vain its momentary fires,
The meteor drops, and in a flash expires.
As one by one, at dread Medea's strain,
The sick'ning stars fade off th'ethereal plain;
As Argus' eyes by Hermes' wand opprest,
Clos'd one by one to everlasting rest;
Thus at her felt approach, and secret might,
Art after art goes out, and all is Night.
See skulking truth to her old cavern fled,
Mountains of Casuistry heap'd o'er her head!
Philosophy, that lean'd on Heav'n before,
Shrinks to her second cause, and is no more.
Physic of Metaphysic begs defence,
And Metaphysic calls for aid on Sense!
See mystery to mathematics fly!
In vain! they gaze, turn giddy, rave, and die.
Religion blushing veils her sacred fires,
And unawares Morality expires.
Nor public flame, nor private, dares to shine;
Nor human spark is left, nor glimpse divine!
Lo! thy dread empire, chaos! is restor'd;
Light dies before thy uncreating word:
Thy hand, great Anarch! lets the curtain fall;
And universal darkness buries all.

52. One of the most
powerful and
individual minds of his
age, Samuel Johnson,
painted by Sir Joshua
Reynolds.

SEVEN

Late Classical Poets and Romantic Pioneers
1750-1805

The practice and example of Pope was supremely influential not only in his own lifetime but for many years afterwards. The Augustan virtues of balance, social decorum, respect for classical precedent, were the criteria by which verse was judged. The couplet (usually the full-scale ten-syllable 'heroic couplet') was the standard form, the point of view often satirical. But technical discipline is not enough in itself, and one sometimes has the feeling, reading many eighteenth-century poems, that the polished surface disguises an emptiness.

This is true at times even in the work of one of the most powerful and individual minds of the age, Samuel Johnson – Dr Johnson. Johnson's main energies certainly did not go into his poetry; but there are parts of his couplet poems, 'London' and 'The Vanity of Human Wishes', which escape slavish respect for Pope, and some poems in quatrain form that have a more distinctly personal feeling, such as 'A Short Song of Congratulation' ('Long-expected one and twenty') and his elegy for his physician and friend, 'On the Death of Dr Robert Levet':

On the Death of Dr Robert Levet

Condemn'd to hope's delusive mine,
As on we toil from day to day,
By sudden blasts, or slow decline,
Our social comforts drop away.

Well tried through many a varying year,
See LEVET to the grave descend;
Officious, innocent, sincere,
Of ev'ry friendless name the friend.

Yet still he fills affection's eye,
Obscurely wise, and coarsely kind;
Nor, letter'd arrogance, deny
Thy praise to merit unrefin'd.

When fainting nature call'd for aid,
And hov'ring death prepar'd the blow,
His vig'rous remedy display'd
The power of art without the show.

In misery's darkest caverns known,
His useful care was ever nigh,
Where hopeless anguish pour'd his groan,
And lonely want retir'd to die.

No summons mock'd by chill delay,
No petty gain disdain'd by pride,
The modest wants of ev'ry day
The toil of every day supplied.

His virtues walk'd their narrow round,
Nor made a pause, nor left a void;
And sure th'Eternal Master found
The single talent well employed.

The busy day, the peaceful night,
Unfelt, uncounted, glided by;
His frame was firm, his powers were bright,
Tho' now his eightieth year was nigh.

Then with no throbbing fiery pain,
No cold gradations of decay,
Death broke at once the vital chain,
And free'd his soul the nearest way.

Out of this late classical or neo-classical period, perhaps one of the few relatively uninteresting periods in all the centuries of English verse, came one of its best-known poems, known at least in odd lines and phrases by many people who probably have no idea where they come from: Thomas Gray's 'An Elegy Written in a Country Churchyard' – often more briefly called 'Gray's Elegy'. Gray was a historian, a Cambridge don, and he was not at all a prolific poet; but a handful of times, and most of all in his 'Elegy', he managed to encapsulate common sentiments about life and death in a way that is both traditional and fresh. Here he finds phrases and cadences which very often seem wholly inevitable. As Dr Johnson said, it 'abounds with images which find a mirror in every mind, and with sentiments to which every bosom returns an echo':

53. Thomas Gray, though not a prolific poet, wrote one of the best known poems in English.

An Elegy Written in a Country Church Yard

The *Curfeu* tolls the Knell of parting Day,
The lowing Herd winds slowly o'er the Lea,
The Plow-man homeward plods his weary Way,
And leaves the World to Darkness and to me.

    Now fades the glimmering Landscape on the Sight,
And all the Air a solemn Stillness holds;
Save where the Beetle wheels his droning Flight,
And drowsy Tinklings lull the distant Folds.

    Save that from yonder Ivy-mantled Tow'r
The mopeing Owl does to the Moon complain
Of such as, wand'ring near her secret Bow'r,
Molest her ancient solitary Reign.

    Beneath whose rugged Elms, that Yew-Tree's Shade,
Where heaves the Turf in many a mould'ring Heap,
Each in his narrow Cell for ever laid,
The rude Forefathers of the Hamlet sleep.

    The breezy Call of Incense-breathing Morn,
The Swallow twitt'ring from the Straw-built Shed,
The Cock's shrill Clarion, or the ecchoing Horn,
No more shall rouse them from their lowly Bed.

    For them no more the blazing Hearth shall burn,
Or busy Houswife ply her Evening Care:
No Children run to lisp their Sire's Return,
Or climb his Knees the envied Kiss to share.

    Oft did the Harvest to their Sickle yield,
Their Furrow oft the stubborn Glebe has broke;
How jocund did they drive their Team afield!
How bow'd the Woods beneath their sturdy Stroke!

    Let not Ambition mock their useful Toil,
Their homely Joys and Destiny obscure;
Nor Grandeur hear with a disdainful Smile,
The short and simple Annals of the Poor.

    The Boast of Heraldry, the Pomp of Pow'r,
And all that Beauty, all that Wealth e'er gave,
Awaits alike th'inevitable Hour.
The Paths of Glory lead but to the Grave.

    Nor you, ye Proud, impute to these the Fault,
If Mem'ry o'er their Tomb no Trophies raise,
Where thro' the long-drawn Isle and fretted Vault
The pealing Anthem swells the Note of Praise.

Can storied Urn or animated Bust
Back to its Mansion call the fleeting Breath?
Can Honour's Voice provoke the silent Dust,
Or Flatt'ry sooth the dull cold Ear of Death?

    Perhaps in this neglected Spot is laid
Some Heart once pregnant with celestial Fire,
Hands that the Rod of Empire might have sway'd,
Or wak'd to Extacy the living Lyre.

    But Knowledge to their Eyes her ample Page
Rich with the Spoils of Time did ne'er unroll;
Chill Penury repress'd their noble Rage,
And froze the genial Current of the Soul.

    Full many a Gem of purest Ray serene,
The dark unfathom'd Caves of Ocean bear:
Full many a Flower is born to blush unseen,
And waste its Sweetness on the desart Air.

    Some Village-*Hampden* that with dauntless Breast
The little Tyrant of his Fields withstood;
Some mute inglorious *Milton* here may rest,
Some *Cromwell* guiltless of his Country's Blood.

    Th'Applause of list'ning Senates to command,
The Threats of Pain and Ruin to despise,
To scatter Plenty o'er a smiling Land,
And read their Hist'ry in a Nation's Eyes

    Their Lot forbad: nor circumscrib'd alone
Their growing Virtues, but their Crimes confin'd;
Forbad to wade through Slaughter to a Throne,
And shut the Gates of Mercy on Mankind,

    The struggling Pangs of conscious Truth to hide,
To quench the Blushes of ingenuous Shame,
Or heap the Shrine of Luxury and Pride
With Incense, kindled at the Muse's Flame.

    Far from the madding Crowd's ignoble Strife,
Their sober Wishes never learn'd to stray;
Along the cool sequester'd Vale of Life
They kept the noiseless Tenor of their Way.

    Yet ev'n these Bones from Insult to protect
Some frail Memorial still erected nigh,
With uncouth Rhimes and shapeless Sculpture deck'd,
Implores the passing Tribute of a Sigh.

    Their Name, their Years, spelt by th'unletter'd Muse,
The Place of Fame and Elegy supply:
And many a holy Text around she strews,
That teach the rustic Moralist to dye.

For who to dumb Forgetfulness a Prey,
This pleasing anxious Being e'er resign'd,
Left the warm Precincts of the chearful Day,
Nor cast one longing ling'ring Look behind?

On some fond Breast the parting Soul relies,
Some pious Drops the closing Eye requires;
Ev'n from the Tomb the Voice of Nature cries,
Ev'n in our Ashes live their wonted Fires.

For thee, who mindful of th'unhonour'd Dead
Dost in these Lines their artless Tale relate;
If chance, by lonely Contemplation led,
Some kindred Spirit shall inquire thy Fate,

Haply some hoary-headed Swain may say,
'Oft have we seen him at the Peep of Dawn
'Brushing with hasty Steps the Dews away
'To meet the Sun upon the upland Lawn.

'There at the Foot of yonder nodding Beech
'That wreathes its old fantastic Roots so high,
'His listless Length at Noontide wou'd he stretch,
'And pore upon the Brook that babbles by.

'Hard by yon Wood, now smiling as in Scorn,
'Mutt'ring his wayward Fancies he wou'd rove,
'Now drooping, woeful wan, like one forlorn,
'Or craz'd with Care, or cross'd in hopeless Love.

'One Morn I miss'd him on the custom'd Hill,
'Along the Heath, and near his fav'rite Tree;
'Another came; nor yet beside the Rill,
'Nor up the Lawn, nor at the Wood was he.

'The next with Dirges due in sad Array
'Slow thro' the Church-way Path we saw him born.
'Approach and read (for thou can'st read) the Lay,
'Grav'd on the Stone beneath yon aged Thorn.'

(There scatter'd oft, the earliest of the Year,
By Hands unseen, are Show'rs of Violets found:
The Red-breast loves to bill and warble there,
And little Footsteps lightly print the Ground.)

The Epitaph

Here rests his Head upon the Lap of Earth
A Youth to Fortune and to Fame unknown:
Fair Science frown'd not on his humble Birth,
And Melancholy mark'd him for her own.

> *Large was his Bounty, and his Soul sincere,*
> *Heav'n did a Recompence as largely send:*
> *He gave to Mis'ry all he had, a Tear:*
> *He gain'd from Heav'n ('twas all he wish'd) a Friend.*
> *   No farther seek his Merits to disclose,*
> *Or draw his Frailties from their dread Abode,*
> *(There they alike in trembling Hope repose)*
> *The Bosom of his Father and his God.*

Towards the end of the eighteenth century, we hear a new note in poetry, a note never heard in the social, reasonable work of the previous epoch. Even when Rochester protested 'Against Reason', he began from a position of rationality. But now there came into circulation new notions of individuality, of freedom and liberty, and of the power of the unfettered imagination. In one direction, these notions led to the American War of Independence and the French Revolution. These historical happenings partly fed on the libertarian writings of Jean-Jacques Rousseau; and it was Rousseau, too, in his persuasive urgings away from social artificiality and back to nature, who influenced poets, novelists and painters to see themselves and the world in a new light. All were part of that difficult-to-define historical impetus called Romanticism.

In the history of the arts, and particularly in the history of poetry, the English can be seen as the pioneers of Romanticism. The earliest pioneers, almost unacknowledged as being of any significance in their own lifetimes, and only slowly recognised long after that, were William Blake and, even earlier, Christopher Smart.

Born in 1722, thirty-five years before Blake, Smart did not become fully appreciated until our own day. He began fairly conventionally, as a don at Cambridge, the writer of decently Miltonic poems on such themes as 'The Attributes of the Supreme Being' which had some small success in their time. But in his late twenties he left Cambridge, with a reputation for being a heavy drinker and rather unstable, and plunged into the rackety and over-worked life of a freelance hack writer.

Gradually bouts of manic behaviour, particularly of religious mania, took over, and towards the end of his life he spent several years in lunatic asylums. There he wrote a great deal, including his finest and strangest poem, 'Jubilate Agno' (Rejoice in the Lamb), which was not published at all until 1939 and not fully available until 1954. 'Jubilate Agno', for all its oddity, is not a work of madness but of celebration. It is a chorus or litany of praise to God for the wonders of his creation – including Smart's own

54. (above) One of the pioneers of Romanticism, Christopher Smart.

55. (below) Smart died insane but wrote his finest poem, 'Jubilate Agno' while in an asylum – not an ideal environment for literary work, as Hogarth's picture of eighteenth-century Bedlam shows.

cat, Jeoffry, to which one whole section is devoted. Years before Blake's famous poem, Smart wrote: 'For the Cherub Cat is a form of the Angel Tiger':

from Jubilate Agno

For I will consider my Cat Jeoffry.

For he is the servant of the Living God, duly and daily serving him.

For at the first glance of the glory of God in the East he worships in his way.

For this is done by wreathing his body seven times round with elegant quickness.

For then he leaps up to catch the musk, which is the blessing of God upon his prayer.

For he rolls upon prank to work it in.

For having done duty and received blessing he begins to consider himself.

For this he performs in ten degrees.

For first he looks upon his fore-paws to see if they are clean.

For secondly he kicks up behind to clear away there.

For thirdly he works it upon stretch with fore-paws extended.

For fourthly he sharpens his paws by wood.

For fifthly he washes himself.

For sixthly he rolls upon wash.

For seventhly he fleas himself, that he may not be interrupted upon the beat.

For eighthly he rubs himself against a post.

For ninthly he looks up for his instructions.

For tenthly he goes in quest of food.

For having consider'd God and himself he will consider his neighbour.

For if he meets another cat he will kiss her in kindness.

For when he takes his prey he plays with it to give it a chance.

For one mouse in seven escapes by his dallying.

For when his day's work is done his business more properly begins.

For he keeps the Lord's watch in the night against the adversary.

For he counteracts the powers of darkness by his electrical skin and glaring eyes.

For he counteracts the Devil, who is death, by brisking about the life.

For in his morning orisons he loves the sun and the sun loves him.

For he is of the tribe of Tiger.

For the Cherub Cat is a term of the Angel Tiger.

For he has the subtlety and hissing of a serpent which in goodness he suppresses.

For he will not do destruction, if he is well-fed neither will he spit without provocation.

For he purrs in thankfulness, when God tells him he's a good Cat.

For he is an instrument for the children to learn benevolence upon.

For every house is incompleat without him and a blessing is lacking in the spirit.

For the Lord commanded Moses concerning the cats at the departure of the Children of Israel from Egypt.

For every family had one cat at least in the bag.

For the English Cats are the best in Europe.

For he is the cleanest in the use of his fore-paws of any quadrupede.

For the dexterity of his defence is an instance of the love of God to him exceedingly.

For he is the quickest to his mark of any creature.

56. 'For the Cherub Cat is a term of the Angel Tiger'. A moulded agateware Staffordshire cat of the eighteenth century.

For he is tenacious of his point.

For he is a mixture of gravity and waggery.

For he knows that God is his Saviour.

For there is nothing sweeter than his peace even at rest.

For there is nothing brisker than his life when in motion.

For he is of the Lord's poor and so indeed is he called by
benevolence perpetually – Poor Jeoffry! poor Jeoffry! the rat
has bit thy throat.

For I bless the name of the Lord Jesus that Jeoffry is better.

For the divine spirit comes about his body to sustain it in
compleat cat.

For his tongue is exceeding pure so that it has in purity what it
wants in musick.

For he is docile and can learn certain things.

For he can set up with gravity which is patience upon
approbation.

For he can fetch and carry, which is patience in employment.

For he can jump over a stick which is patience upon proof
positive.

For he can spraggle upon waggle at the word of command.

For he can jump from an eminence into his master's bosom.

For he can catch the cork and toss it again.

For he is hated by the hypocrite and miser.

For the former is afraid of detection.

For the latter refuses the charge.

For he camels his back to bear the first notion of business.

For he is good to think on, if a man would express himself
neatly.

For he was made a great figure in Egypt for his signal services.

For he killed the Icneumon-rat very pernicious by land.

For his ears are so acute that they sting again.

For from this proceeds the passing quickness of his attention.

For by stroaking of him I have found out electricity.

For I perceived God's light about him both wax and fire.

For the Electrical fire is the spiritual substance, which God sends
from heaven to sustain the bodies both of man and beast.

For God has blessed him in the variety of his movements.

For, tho he cannot fly, he is an excellent clamberer.

For his motions upon the face of the earth are more than any
other quadrupede.

For he can tread to all the measures upon the musick.

For he can swim for life.

For he can creep.

For many years it was commonplace to call William Blake mad too, as if that settled the matter – a genius, but mad. He was ignored by his fellow poets on the whole, though on the news of his death in 1827 the critic Crabb Robinson was moved to remark, 'There is no doubt this poor man was mad, but there is something in the madness of this man which interests me more than the sanity of Lord Byron or Walter Scott!'

57. William Blake, drawn on Hampstead Heath, was regarded during his lifetime as a genius but mad.

In Blake's best-known poem, 'The Tyger', Smart's loving, exuberant, eccentric itemising of one particular creature is concentrated into something emblematic. Blake's poems are emblems in a double sense; because alongside them, as part of the whole design, Blake made copper etchings which he then coloured by hand, the whole series making up two books. He wanted those who looked at them, and looked into them, to have a total experience, to be both readers and spectators. Blake's 'Tyger' – one of that group he called *Songs of Experience*, as opposed to his *Songs of Innocence* – is a very naked confrontation with one of God's many puzzles. Did God create power and evil as well as gentleness and good?

The Tyger

Tyger, tyger, burning bright
In the forests of the night,
What immortal hand or eye
Could frame thy fearful symmetry?

In what distant deeps or skies
Burnt the fire of thine eyes?
On what wings dare he aspire?
What the hand dare seize the fire?

And what shoulder and what art
Could twist the sinews of thy heart?
And, when thy heart began to beat,
What dread hand and what dread feet?

What the hammer? What the chain?
In what furnace was thy brain?
What the anvil? What dread grasp
Dare its deadly terrors clasp?

When the stars threw down their spears,
And water'd heaven with their tears,
Did He smile His work to see?
Did He who made the lamb make thee?

Tyger, tyger, burning bright
In the forests of the night,
What immortal hand or eye
Dare frame thy fearful symmetry?

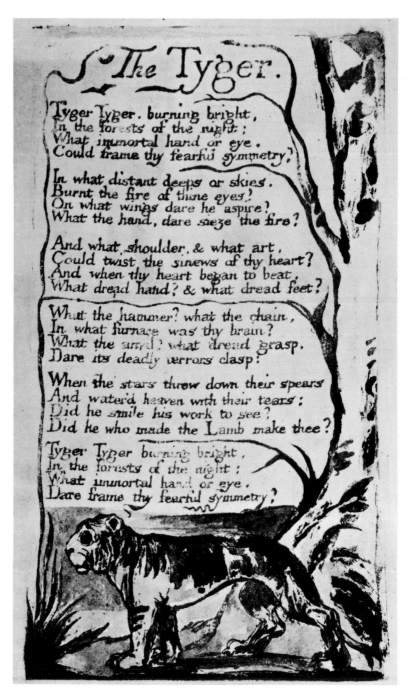

58. Blake illustrated *Songs of Experience* himself; this is the 'Tyger' page.

Blake gave a subtitle to his *Songs of Innocence and Experience*: 'Shewing the Two Contrary States of the Human Soul'. The tiger and the lamb are equal and opposite products of God's creation, twins in the paradox of life. At one level, the level of extreme simplicity, Blake wrote the *Songs of Innocence*. They are poems so clear and transparent, like 'Holy Thursday', that often they feel like anonymous children's songs, lyrics that have been there from the beginning:

Holy Thursday

'Twas on a Holy Thursday, their innocent faces clean,
The children walking two and two, in red and blue and
 green,
Grey-headed beadles walk'd before, with wands as white
 as snow,
Till into the high dome of Paul's they like Thames'
 waters flow.

O what a multitude they seem'd, these flowers of
 London Town!
Seated in companies they sit with radiance all their own.
The hum of multitudes was there, but multitudes of
 lambs,
Thousands of little boys and girls raising their innocent
 hands.

Now like a mighty wind they raise to Heaven the voice
 of song,
Or like harmonious thunderings the seats of Heaven
 among.
Beneath them sit the agèd men, wise guardians of the
 poor;
Then cherish pity, lest you drive an angel from your
 door.

That poem from *Songs of Innocence* is balanced by one with exactly the same title from *Songs of Experience*, which begins:

Is this a holy thing to see
In a rich and fruitful land,
Babes reduced to misery,
Fed with cold and usurous hand?

> Is that trembling cry a song?
> Can it be a song of joy?
> And so many children poor?
> It is a land of poverty!

But the 'contrary states' can sometimes be alleviated, if not wholly reconciled. For example, in his poem 'London' – on the face of it one of Blake's grimmest – a beam of light illuminates the boy in the engraving as he leads the old man 'thro' each charter'd street':

London

> I wander thro' each charter'd street,
> Near where the charter'd Thames doth flow,
> And mark in every face I meet
> Marks of weakness, marks of woe.
>
> In ev'ry cry of every Man,
> In ev'ry Infant's cry of fear,
> In every voice, in every ban,
> The mind-forg'd manacles I hear.
>
> How the Chimney-sweeper's cry
> Every black'ning Church appalls;
> And the hapless Soldier's sigh
> Runs in blood down Palace walls.
>
> But most thro' midnight streets I hear
> How the youthful Harlot's curse
> Blasts the new born Infant's tear
> And blights with plagues the Marriage hearse.

Much of Blake's poetry is a plea for openness, for honesty, for acceptance of true feeling: as he wrote in 'The Marriage of Heaven and Hell', 'For every thing that lives is holy'. This too is part of what we mean by Romanticism, and in Blake's case it comes across with a mystical simplicity, a psychological plainness about human complexities that sometimes seems to anticipate Freudian analysis more than a hundred years before it existed. An example is his poem 'A Poison Tree', which is like a fable about emotional repression:

59. Blake's dramatic pictures for 'A Poison Tree' from *Songs of Experience.*

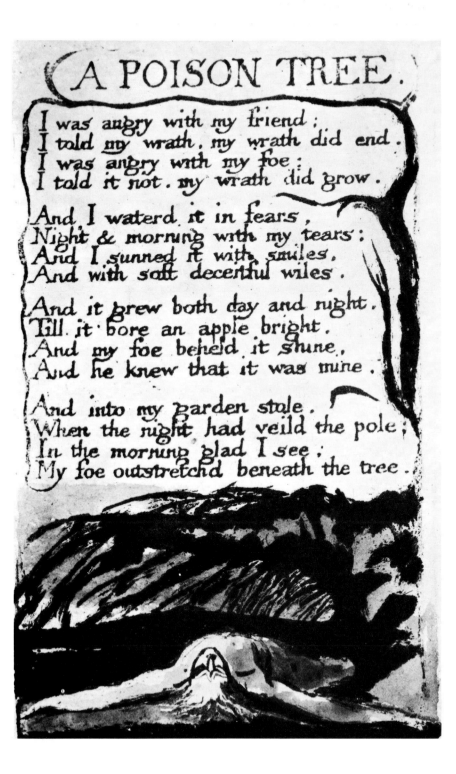

A POISON TREE.

I was angry with my friend;
I told my wrath, my wrath did end.
I was angry with my foe:
I told it not, my wrath did grow.

And I waterd it in fears,
Night & morning with my tears:
And I sunned it with smiles,
And with soft deceitful wiles.

And it grew both day and night,
Till it bore an apple bright.
And my foe beheld it shine,
And he knew that it was mine,

And into my garden stole,
When the night had veild the pole;
In the morning glad I see;
My foe outstretchd beneath the tree.

A Poison Tree

I was angry with my friend:
I told my wrath, my wrath did end.
I was angry with my foe:
I told it not, my wrath did grow.

And I water'd it in fears,
Night and morning with my tears;
And I sunnèd it with smiles,
And with soft deceitful wiles.

And it grew both day and night,
Till it bore an apple bright;
And my foe beheld it shine,
And he knew that it was mine,

And into my garden stole
When the night had veil'd the pole:
In the morning glad I see
My foe outstretch'd beneath the tree.

In 'The Clod and the Pebble', St Paul's words about Love from the Epistle to the Corinthians are again put into the form of a fable or parable, in which what the clod of clay says and what the pebble says coexist as Innocence and Experience coexist. Blake was a master of the aphorism, the paradoxical proverb, by-passing reason and all kinds of religious orthodoxy:

The Clod and the Pebble

'Love seeketh not Itself to please,
'Nor for itself hath any care,
'But for another gives its ease,
'And builds a Heaven in Hell's despair.'

So sung a little Clod of Clay
Trodden with the cattle's feet,
But a Pebble of the brook
Warbled out these metres meet:

'Love seeketh only Self to please,
'To bind another to Its delight,
'Joys in another's loss of ease,
'And builds a hell in Heaven's despite.'

But, as I have suggested, William Blake was an isolated figure, a prophet and mystic who had almost no influence at all on his contemporaries, and very little on his successors until our own century. His later poems, the difficult messages of such 'Prophetic Books' as

60. Blake had almost no influence on his contemporaries and wrote as a dedicated and lonely poet without an audience.

'Jerusalem' and 'Milton', came out of that extreme isolation – the work of a dedicated and lonely man without an audience. But there were other writers of his time and in the following generation who, without really knowing him or his work, were more immediately and effectively changing habitual attitudes to art in general and poetry in particular.

In 1798 two men in their late twenties published together anonymously a book which quite consciously set out to demonstrate a new way. William Wordsworth, from Cumberland, and Samuel Taylor Coleridge, from Devon – both educated at Cambridge – had met shortly before; and together they planned *Lyrical Ballads*. As Coleridge years later described what they were after, he wrote that Wordsworth's object was 'to give the charm of novelty to things of everyday, and to excite a feeling analogous to the supernatural, by awakening the mind's attention from the lethargy of custom, and directing it to the loveliness and the wonders of the world before us'. Coleridge said of himself that his own 'endeavours should be directed to persons and characters supernatural, or at least romantic' –

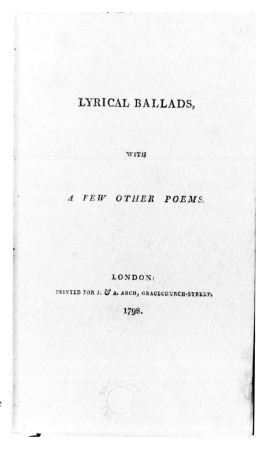

LYRICAL BALLADS,

WITH

A FEW OTHER POEMS.

LONDON:

PRINTED FOR J. & A. ARCH, GRACECHURCH-STREET,

1798.

61. The title page of *Lyrical Ballads*, published jointly and anonymously by Coleridge and Wordsworth in an attempt to demonstrate a new approach to poetry.

that is, in the meaning Coleridge intended, *inventive, imaginative*. In the *Lyrical Ballads*, Coleridge's chief contribution was 'The Rime of the Ancient Mariner', an extraordinary symbolic imitation of a traditional ballad, full of odd details gathered from his reading of books of adventurous travel and voyages.

But in that same year, 1798, Coleridge wrote another poem, not to be published until several years later, the circumstances of which he surrounded with a mystery that has become a legend: 'Kubla Khan'. He sub-titled it 'A Vision in a Dream'. His account of how he wrote it tells of sitting in his cottage on the Somerset–Devon borders, taking 'an anodyne' as he calls it (probably laudanum, to which he became addicted) because he felt ill, and thus falling asleep while he was reading a seventeenth-century book. He says he slept for three hours, and was aware of dreaming two or three hundred lines which, when he woke, he began to transcribe – until, he says,

> at this moment he was unfortunately called out by a person on business from Porlock, and detained by him above an hour, and on his return to his room, found, to his no small surprise and mortification, that though he still retained some vague and dim recollection of the general purpose of the vision, yet, with the exception of some eight or ten scattered lines and images, all the rest had passed away like the images on the surface of a stream into which a stone has been cast . . .

Doubt has been thrown on whether this is an entirely true account of the poem's composition: the poem itself draws most subtly and strangely on Coleridge's wide reading. But its force is very much that of the sub-title, 'A Vision in a Dream'. He also calls it 'a Fragment'; but it could be said that a great deal of Romantic poetry is fragmentary – the connections are left to us:

Kubla Khan

In Xanadu did Kubla Khan
A stately pleasure-dome decree:
Where Alph, the sacred river, ran
Through caverns measureless to man
   Down to a sunless sea.
So twice five miles of fertile ground
With walls and towers were girdled round:
And there were gardens bright with sinuous rills,
Where blossomed many an incense-bearing tree,
And here were forests ancient as the hills,
Enfolding sunny spots of greenery.

But oh! that deep romantic chasm which slanted
Down the green hill athwart a cedarn cover!
A savage place! as holy and enchanted
As e'er beneath a waning moon was haunted
By woman wailing for her demon-lover!

62. Samuel Coleridge
in 1795, three years
before the publication
of *Lyrical Ballads* and
the writing of 'Kubla
Khan'.

And from this chasm, with ceaseless turmoil seething,
As if this earth in fast thick pants were breathing,
A mighty fountain momently was forced:
Amid whose swift half-intermitted burst
Huge fragments vaulted like rebounding hail,
Or chaffy grain beneath the thresher's flail:
And 'mid these dancing rocks at once and ever
It flung up momently the sacred river.
Five miles meandering with a mazy motion
Through wood and dale the sacred river ran,
Then reached the caverns measureless to man,
And sank in tumult to a lifeless ocean:
And 'mid this tumult Kubla heard from far
Ancestral voices prophesying war!

   The shadow of the dome of pleasure
   Floated midway on the waves;
   Where was heard the mingled measure
   From the fountain and the caves.
It was a miracle of rare device,
A sunny pleasure-dome with caves of ice!

   A damsel with a dulcimer
   In a vision once I saw:
   It was an Abyssinian maid,
   And on her dulcimer she played,
   Singing of Mount Abora.
   Could I revive within me
   Her symphony and song,
   To such a deep delight 'twould win me,
   That with music loud and long,
   I would build that dome in air,
   That sunny dome! those caves of ice!
   And all who heard should see them there,
   And all should cry, Beware! Beware!
   His flashing eyes, his floating hair!
   Weave a circle round him thrice,
   And close your eyes with holy dread,
   For he on honey-dew hath fed,
   And drunk the milk of Paradise.

EIGHT

Wordsworth
1770 - 1850

Coleridge's remark, which I quoted in the last section, about Wordsworth's task in *Lyrical Ballads* being to direct the mind 'to the loveliness and the wonders of the world before us', gives only a partial view of what Wordsworth achieved in his long writing life. He was certainly a more prolific and important poet than Coleridge; he was also more complex, not at all the simple or silly caricature first invented by

63. Wordsworth, referring to his own method of work, described poetry as 'emotion recollected in tranquillity'.

Byron. In the preface he wrote to the 1800 second edition of *Lyrical Ballads*, he spoke of 'emotion recollected in tranquillity' – a form of words which has sometimes been taken to be a definition of what poetry is. Rather, it was an observation of Wordsworth's own method of work as he saw it at the time. But the actual sources of his poetry seem to be more complicated than simply emotions recollected or scenes recorded.

Take, for example, his poem 'The Solitary Reaper'. In 1803 Wordsworth went on a tour of Scotland. He was fascinated by hearing Gaelic spoken, a language which of course he could not understand. Two years later, he wrote 'The Solitary Reaper'. But Wordsworth's Quaker friend Thomas Wilkinson had also visited the Scottish Highlands, and had written an account of his travels, not published till many years later, but which he circulated among his friends. In that prose journal, Wilkinson recorded just such an encounter with a girl singing in Gaelic in the fields, and he noted that the strains of the music 'felt delicious long after they were heard no more'. In Wordsworth's poem, a personal memory and someone else's experience blended together, making something circumstantial into something visionary:

The Solitary Reaper

Behold her, single in the field,
Yon solitary Highland Lass!
Reaping and singing by herself;
Stop here, or gently pass!
Alone she cuts and binds the grain,
And sings a melancholy strain;
O listen! for the Vale profound
Is overflowing with the sound.

No Nightingale did ever chaunt
More welcome notes to weary bands
Of travellers in some shady haunt,
Among Arabian sands:
A voice so thrilling ne'er was heard
In spring-time from the Cuckoo-bird,
Breaking the silence of the seas
Among the farthest Hebrides.

Will no one tell me what she sings? –
Perhaps the plaintive numbers flow
For old, unhappy, far-off things,
And battles long ago:

64. (above) 'Behold her, single in the field,
Yon solitary Highland Lass?'

65. (right) This
painting of Grasmere
in 1806, by the
Wordsworths' friend
Ibbetson, shows
Allan Bank, where
they moved in 1808.

Or is it some more humble lay,
Familiar matter of to-day?
Some natural sorrow, loss, or pain,
That has been, and may be again?

Whate'er the theme, the Maiden sang
As if her song could have no ending;
I saw her singing at her work,
And o'er the sickle bending; –
I listened, motionless and still;
And, as I mounted up the hill,
The music in my heart I bore,
Long after it was heard no more.

The label that has always been hung round Wordsworth's neck is one
that reads 'Nature Poet'. Generations of schoolchildren have been
brought up on his poem 'The Daffodils', and some people tend to
suppose that most of Wordsworth is to do with flowers and hills and lakes,
a sort of Lake District of the mind, full of the beauties of inanimate
nature, with actual human beings rather thin on the ground. The fact that
Wordsworth is thought of in this way is partly attributable to Wordsworth
himself: after all, he did call himself a 'Worshipper of Nature'. But the
real force, the powerful strangeness, of his poetry at its best comes

66. (above) This silhouette is the only portrait of Dorothy Wordsworth, the poet's devoted sister.

67. (below) The entry in Dorothy Wordsworth's journal for 15 April 1802, referring to daffodils by the shore of Ullswater.

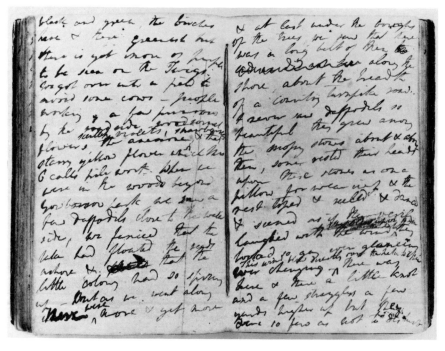

through because we are made aware of the *human* side of nature: of human nature as well as inanimate nature, and of man as an instrument through which nature transmits its messages.

Such a vision could come to Wordsworth even in the middle of what was then the biggest city in the world. In the summer of 1802, early in the morning of 31 July, he and his sister Dorothy crossed Westminster Bridge on the top of the coach from London to Dover. A month later, at Dove Cottage by Grasmere, he wrote the words:

Upon Westminster Bridge

Earth has not anything to show more fair:
Dull would he be of soul who could pass by
A sight so touching in its majesty:
This City now doth like a garment wear
The beauty of the morning; silent, bare,
Ships, towers, domes, theatres, and temples lie
Open unto the fields, and to the sky;
All bright and glittering in the smokeless air.
Never did sun more beautifully steep
In his first splendour valley, rock, or hill;
Ne'er saw I, never felt, a calm so deep!
The river glideth at his own sweet will:
Dear God! the very houses seem asleep;
And all that mighty heart is lying still!

His sister Dorothy was his closest lifelong companion. Reading her journal, time and again we find Dorothy noting exactly the scenes and the incidents which her brother would transform in his poems, as in the sonnet on Westminster Bridge and in 'The Daffodils'. Walking home by Ullswater one day in April 1802, William and Dorothy were struck by the sight of a long, broad belt of daffodils by the lake shore. Dorothy wrote about them straightaway in her journal for that day, 15 April. Two years later – again 'emotion recollected in tranquillity' – Wordsworth turned the experience into something not only visionary but solitary:

The Daffodils

I wander'd lonely as a cloud
That floats on high o'er vales and hills,
When all at once I saw a crowd,
A host of golden daffodils,
Beside the lake, beneath the trees,
Fluttering and dancing in the breeze.

Continuous as the stars that shine
And twinkle on the milky way,
They stretch'd in never-ending line
Along the margin of a bay;
Ten thousand saw I at a glance
Tossing their heads in sprightly dance.

The waves beside them danced, but they
Out-did the sparkling waves in glee: –
A Poet could not but be gay
In such a jocund company!
I gazed – and gazed – but little thought
What wealth the show to me had brought;

For oft, when on my couch I lie
In vacant or in pensive mood,
They flash upon that inward eye
Which is the bliss of solitude;
And then my heart with pleasure fills,
And dances with the daffodils.

A few years earlier, during the bitterly severe winter months of 1798–9, Wordsworth and Dorothy were together in Germany, living cheaply and trying to learn German so that they could be employed as translators. It was not a happy time, but Wordsworth was then at work writing some of his most enduring poems.

First, there was his enigmatic group of so-called *Lucy* poems: short elegiac lyrics which seem to be concerned with the death of a young, beautiful, completely natural and spontaneous girl. The identity of 'Lucy' has puzzled generations of scholars and commentators. Was she a lost love of his childhood? Is she in some sense an imagined version of Dorothy? Coleridge commented on the poems in a letter to a friend: 'Whether it had any reality I cannot say. Most probably, in some gloomier moment he had fancied the moment when his sister might die'. Whatever the answer – and we shall probably never know – these eight lines make a powerful and passionate memorial:

A slumber did my spirit seal

A slumber did my spirit seal;
   I had no human fears:
She seem'd a thing that could not feel
   The touch of earthly years.

No motion has she now, no force;
   She neither hears nor sees;
Roll'd round in earth's diurnal course
   With rocks, and stones, and trees.

The other poem Wordsworth began during that German winter when he was in his late twenties was something much longer, something at the very centre of his life, and something which occupied him for much of the rest of that life. It was not in fact published until two months after his death in 1850; and, though he had substantially finished it forty-five years earlier, he had gone back to it and revised it ever afterwards. This major work was what became known as *The Prelude*; but Wordsworth himself gave it other names, which eventually were used as its sub-titles – 'The Growth of a Poet's Mind, an Autobiographical Poem'.

Without knowing what it was to become, in a mood of physical depression and mental uncertainty, Wordsworth in Germany began to explore his own beginnings, his free and happy childhood in Cumberland, and what he called those 'spots of time' which lingered in his memory as moments of visionary strength. And these are always the moments of Wordsworth's greatest strength as a poet, when he moves exaltedly, even excitedly, from the circumstantial, when his memory catches fire.

The germ of part of *The Prelude* can be seen in a poem written when he was twenty-nine, with the weighty and rather off-putting title 'Influence of Natural Objects in Calling Forth and Strengthening the Imagination in Boyhood and Early Youth'. This was first published in a magazine edited by Coleridge, and it began with the line 'Wisdom and Spirit of the Universe!' The earlier lines, up to and including the description of taking the boat out and being frightened, came later.

But *The Prelude* as a whole, as we read it now, is a very carefully unified poem, taking Wordsworth from his boyhood and schooldays, through his student days in Cambridge, his journey through the Alps, his time in

London and his time in France, down to his rediscovery of powers of imagination and spiritual strength which he thought he had lost. In a way, it is a poem about Paradise, about its loss and its regaining, which follows reverently but highly originally in the footsteps of Milton:

from The Prelude, Book I

Dust as we are, the immortal spirit grows
Like harmony in music; there is a dark
Inscrutable workmanship that reconciles
Discordant elements, makes them cling together
In one society. How strange that all
The terrors, pains, and early miseries,
Regrets, vexations, lassitudes interfused
Within my mind, should e'er have borne a part,
And that a needful part, in making up
The calm existence that is mine when I
Am worthy of myself! Praise to the end!
Thanks to the means which Nature deigned to employ;
Whether her fearless visitings, or those
That came with soft alarm, like hurtless light
Opening the peaceful clouds; or she may use
Severer interventions, ministry
More palpable, as best might suit her aim.

One summer evening (led by her) I found
A little boat tied to a willow tree
Within a rocky cave, its usual home.
Straight I unloosed her chain, and stepping in
Pushed from the shore. It was an act of stealth
And troubled pleasure, nor without the voice
Of mountain-echoes did my boat move on;
Leaving behind her still, on either side,
Small circles glittering idly in the moon,
Until they melted all into one track
Of sparkling light. But now, like one who rows,
Proud of his skill, to reach a chosen point
With an unswerving line, I fixed my view
Upon the summit of a craggy ridge,
The horizon's utmost boundary; for above
Was nothing but the stars and the grey sky.
She was an elfin pinnace; lustily

68. (above)
Wordsworth
drawn in 1818,
looking almost
Byronic, by Haydon.

69. (below)
Wordsworth recalled
his days at St John's
College, Cambridge,
in his
autobiographical
poem, 'The Prelude'.

I dipped my oars into the silent lake,
And, as I rose upon the stroke, my boat
Went heaving through the water like a swan;
When, from behind that craggy steep till then
The horizon's bound, a huge peak, black and huge,
As if with voluntary power instinct
Upreared its head. I struck and struck again,
And growing still in stature the grim shape
Towered up between me and the stars, and still,
For so it seemed, with purpose of its own
And measured motion like a living thing,
Strode after me. With trembling oars I turned,
And through the silent water stole my way
Back to the covert of the willow tree;
There in her mooring-place I left my bark –
And through the meadows homeward went, in grave
And serious mood; but after I had seen
That spectacle, for many days, my brain
Worked with a dim and undetermined sense
Of unknown modes of being; o'er my thoughts
There hung a darkness, call it solitude
Or blank desertion. No familiar shapes
Remained, no pleasant images of trees,
Of sea or sky, no colours of green fields;
But huge and mighty forms, that do not live
Like living men, moved slowly through the mind
By day, and were a trouble to my dreams.

Wisdom and Spirit of the universe!
Thou Soul that art the eternity of thought,
That givest to forms and images a breath
And everlasting motion, not in vain
By day or star-light thus from my first dawn
Of childhood didst thou interwine for me
The passions that build up our human soul;
Not with the mean and vulgar works of man,
But with high objects, with enduring things –
With life and nature – purifying thus
The elements of feeling and of thought,
And sanctifying, by such discipline,
Both pain and fear, until we recognise
A grandeur in the beatings of the heart.
Nor was this fellowship vouchsafed to me
With stinted kindness. In November days,

When vapours rolling down the valley made
A lonely scene more lonesome, among woods,
At noon and 'mid the calm of summer nights,
When, by the margin of the trembling lake,
Beneath the gloomy hills homeward I went
In solitude, such intercourse was mine;
Mine was it in the fields both day and night,
And by the waters, all the summer long.

And in the frosty season, when the sun
Was set, and visible for many a mile
The cottage windows blazed through twilight gloom,
I heeded not their summons: happy time
It was indeed for all of us – for me
It was a time of rapture! Clear and loud
The village clock tolled six, – I wheeled about,
Proud and exulting like an untired horse
That cares not for his home. All shod with steel,
We hissed along the polished ice in games
Confederate, imitative of the chase
And woodland pleasures, – the resounding horn,
The pack hound chiming, and the hunted hare.
So through the darkness and the cold we flew,
And not a voice was idle; with the din
Smitten, the precipices rang aloud;
The leafless trees and every icy crag
Tinkled like iron; while far distant hills
Into the tumult sent an alien sound
Of melancholy not unnoticed, while the stars
Eastward were sparkling clear, and in the west
The orange sky of evening died away.
Not seldom from the uproar I retired
Into a silent bay, or sportively
Glanced sideway, leaving the tumultuous throng,
To cut across the reflex of a star
That fled, and, flying still before me, gleamed
Upon the glassy plain; and oftentimes,
When we had given our bodies to the wind,
And all the shadowy banks on either side
Came sweeping through the darkness, spinning still
The rapid line of motion, then at once
Have I, reclining back upon my heels,
Stopped short; yet still the solitary cliffs
Wheeled by me – even as if the earth had rolled

With visible motion her diurnal round!
Behind me did they stretch in solemn train,
Feebler and feebler, and I stood and watched
Till all was tranquil as a dreamless sleep.

Wordsworth said of *The Prelude* – indeed, of his work in general – that it was 'a thing unprecedented in literary history that a man should talk so much about himself'. But he was not just an impregnable solitary. Apart from Dorothy, there was his wife Mary, to whom he wrote many tender

70. Wordsworth's wife Mary, whom he married in 1802.

and loving letters which have only quite recently been discovered and published; there were his five much-loved children; and there were many friends – literary people and non-literary people alike. Surviving until he was eighty years old, he outlived most of them; and went on writing, though he seldom regained the power of those ten marvellous years between about 1797 and 1807 when he wrote his best work.

But much later than that, in his sixty-sixth year, at Rydal Mount (his home from 1815 until his death), he was stirred into moving eloquence by

71. A watercolour of Rydal Mount, Wordsworth's home from 1815 until his death in 1850.

the death of an old friend. In 1835 James Hogg died – 'the Ettrick Shepherd', as he was known, and indeed he was born in Ettrick Forest in Scotland and had worked as a shepherd. Hogg had been taken up by the novelist and poet Walter Scott, and had made the acquaintance, sometimes the friendship, of many literary notables in the 1810s and 1820s, including Wordsworth.

Wordsworth and Hogg had been born in the same year, 1770, and on Hogg's death Wordsworth wrote what he called 'An Extempore Effusion'. In it, he commemorates not only Hogg but Scott, Coleridge, Charles Lamb the essayist and George Crabbe the poet – writers, all now dead, who had been his friends. Wordsworth speaks as a 'frail survivor'. By this time, too, the finest poets of the generation that followed him (Shelley, Keats and Byron, who fall into the next section) had all died young. It is a poignant moment in an old man's life:

An Extempore Effusion

When first, descending from the moorlands,
I saw the stream of Yarrow glide
Along a bare and open valley,
The Ettrick Shepherd was my guide.

When last along its banks I wandered,
Through groves that had begun to shed
Their golden leaves upon the pathways,
My steps the Border-minstrel led.

The mighty Minstrel breathes no longer,
'Mid mouldering ruins low he lies;
And death upon the braes of Yarrow,
Has closed the Shepherd-poet's eyes:

Nor has the rolling year twice measured,
From sign to sign, its steadfast course,
Since every mortal power of Coleridge
Was frozen at its marvellous source;

The rapt One, of the godlike forehead,
The heaven-eyed creature sleeps in earth:
And Lamb, the frolic and the gentle,
Has vanished from his lonely hearth.

Like clouds that rake the mountain-summits,
Or waves that own no curbing hand,
How fast has brother followed brother,
From sunshine to the sunless land!

Yet I, whose lids from infant slumber
Were earlier raised, remain to hear
A timid voice, that asks in whispers,
'Who next will drop and disappear?'

Our haughty life is crowned with darkness,
Like London with its own black wreath,
On which with thee, O Crabbe! forth-looking,
I gazed from Hampstead's breezy heath.

72. Wordsworth regarded this
1842 portrait, again by Haydon,
as the best, most characteristic
likeness of himself.

As if but yesterday departed,
Thou too art gone before; but why,
O'er ripe fruit, seasonably gathered,
Should frail survivors heave a sigh?

Mourn rather for that holy spirit,
Sweet as the spring, as ocean deep;
For her who, ere her summer faded,
Has sunk into a breathless sleep.

No more of old romantic sorrows,
For slaughtered youth or love-lorn maid!
With sharper grief is Yarrow smitten,
And Ettrick mourns with her their poet dead.

James Hogg

73. Wordsworth's old friend,
James Hogg, 'the Ettrick Shepherd',
who died in 1835.

NINE

Younger Romantics
1800-24

In the years following the conclusion of the Napoleonic Wars in 1815, there was much political unrest in England. King George III, who was to die in 1820, had been insane for most of the century, while his cynical and pleasure-loving son (later George IV) was Prince Regent. The government ministers were repressive, frightened of possible revolution. Percy Shelley was indeed a revolutionary, and an atheist as well. In a sonnet written in 1819, he put much of his feeling of impotent rage, despair and loathing into such lines as these, a portrait of the England he saw:

> An old, mad, blind, despised, and dying king –
> Princes, the dregs of their dull race, who flow
> Through public scorn – mud from a muddy spring . . .

It was his vitriolic but limited response to what he saw as a decaying tyranny. But a little earlier, in another sonnet, he took a longer view, equally tersely expressed but facing with ironical relief the distancing of history – facing the certainty that these things will pass, the poem itself becoming a monument to such certainty. At the beginning of 'Ozymandias', Shelley says 'I met a traveller from an antique land'; but in fact he had been reading a book by an ancient Greek historian (Diodorus Siculus, a contemporary of Julius Caesar). In it he had found a description of a monument erected by an Egyptian monarch, with a version of the inscription he quotes in the poem:

Ozymandias

I met a traveller from an antique land,
Who said: Two vast and trunkless legs of stone
Stand in the desert. Near them, on the sand,
Half sunk, a shattered visage lies, whose frown
And wrinkled lip and sneer of cold command,
Tell that its sculptor well those passions read,

74. (above) George III, described by Shelley as 'An old, mad, blind, despised and dying king'.

75. (below) The best authenticated portrait of Shelley, painted in Rome, 1819, by Amelia Curran.

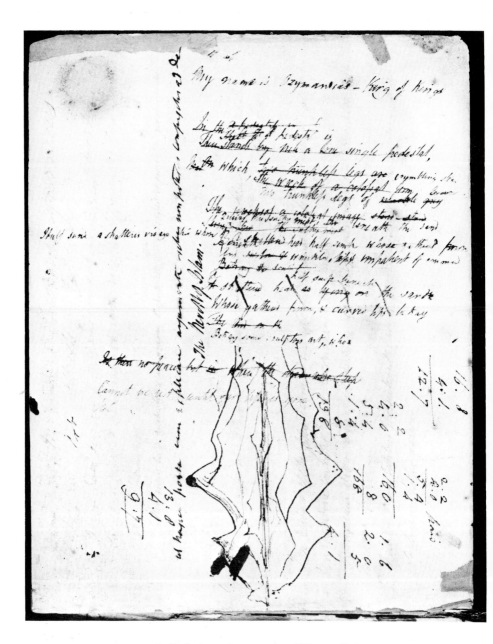

76. Shelley's rough manuscript of 'Ozymandias'.

Which yet survive stamped on these lifeless things,
The hand that mocked them, and the heart that fed:
And on the pedestal these words appear:
'My name is Ozymandias, King of Kings:
Look on my works, ye Mighty, and despair!'
Nothing beside remains. Round the decay
Of that colossal wreck, boundless and bare
The lone and level sands stretch far away.

Shelley was twenty-five when he wrote 'Ozymandias'. He was impulsive, highly intellectual as well as emotional, a radical in all things. Many of the notions that still float about today of the poet as rebel, martyr, impractical dreamer, are based on concepts of Shelley or ideas (sometimes mistaken ideas) about him. Like Keats, he died in Italy; like Keats and Byron, he died young. But Shelley had a tougher side to him than he is sometimes given credit for, as in his revolutionary ballad 'The Mask of Anarchy'.

77. Shelley in Rome
at the Baths of Caracalla.

One of the manifestations of the post-Napoleonic reactionary regimes across Europe (Metternich's in Austria, Castlereagh's in England) was a reliance on brutal martial law. In 1818, the year after Shelley wrote 'Ozymandias', troops in Manchester were ordered to fire into a peaceful working-class meeting – which became known as the Peterloo Massacre. Shelley's fierce reaction to that incident can be seen in 'The Mask of Anarchy', in which from his self-exile in Italy he names names (Castlereagh, Eldon, Sidmouth), and finally turns it into a revolutionary hymn. What follows are the first nine stanzas of the poem, and then the final two:

from The Mask of Anarchy

As I lay asleep in Italy
There came a voice from over the Sea,
And with great power it forth led me
To walk in the visions of Poesy.

I met Murder on the way –
He had a mask like Castlereagh –
Very smooth he looked, yet grim;
Seven blood-hounds followed him:

All were fat; and well they might
Be in admirable plight,
For one by one, and two by two,
He tossed them human hearts to chew
Which from his wide cloak he drew.

Next came Fraud, and he had on,
Like Eldon, an ermined gown;
His big tears, for he wept well,
Turned to mill-stones as they fell.

And the little children, who
Round his feet played to and fro,
Thinking every tear a gem,
Had their brains knocked out by them.

Clothed with the Bible, as with light,
And the shadows of the night,
Like Sidmouth, next, Hypocrisy
On a crocodile rode by.

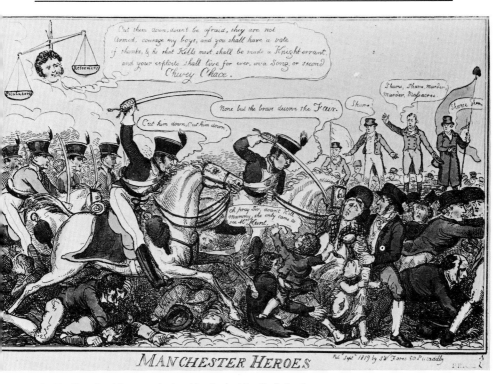

78. The Peterloo Massacre depicted by the satirist Cruikshank:
the yeomanry charges the mob.

And many more Destructions played
In this ghastly masquerade,
All disguised, even to the eyes,
Like Bishops, lawyers, peers, or spies.

Last came Anarchy: he rode
On a white horse, splashed with blood;
He was pale even to the lips,
Like Death in the Apocalypse.

And he wore a kingly crown;
And in his grasp a sceptre shone;
On his brow this mark I saw –
'I AM GOD, AND KING, AND LAW!'

       *   *   *

'And these words shall then become
Like Oppression's thundered doom
Ringing through each heart and brain,
Heard again – again – again –

'Rise like Lions after slumber
In unvanquishable number –
Shake your chains to earth like dew
Which in sleep had fallen on you –
Ye are many – they are few.'

The five years between 1820 and 1825 saw the deaths in succession of Keats, Shelley and Byron. John Keats, the youngest of the three, came from much the least privileged background: his father looked after horses at a London inn, both his parents died while he was a child, and with some struggle he managed to qualify in medicine. Soon after this, within a short time, his early poems had so impressed the most brilliant and controversial literary editor of the time, Leigh Hunt, that Hunt encouraged him to concentrate on poetry. Keats met Wordsworth, by now very grand and famous, and Shelley, who invited him to Italy to try to cure the tuberculosis he had developed.

Towards the end of 1820 Keats indeed set off for Italy; but it was too late. Within three months of his arrival, he died, aged twenty-five. For many years, it was supposed that the following sonnet was Keats's last poem, because he wrote it out for a friend during the voyage to Italy. It is now known that it was written in 1819. But it can stand as Keats's self-elegy, combining as it does his habitual themes of love and death:

Bright star, would I were stedfast as thou art –
   Not in lone splendour hung aloft the night
And watching, with eternal lids apart,
   Like Nature's patient, sleepless Eremite,
The moving waters at their priestlike task
   Of pure ablution round earth's human shores,
Or gazing on the new soft-fallen mask
   Of snow upon the mountains and the moors –
No – yet still stedfast, still unchangeable,
   Pillow'd upon my fair love's ripening breast,
To feel for ever its soft fall and swell,
   Awake for ever in a sweet unrest,
Still, still to hear her tender-taken breath,
And so live ever – or else swoon to death.

79. Keats captured vividly in a pen-and-ink drawing of 1816.

Within the year of Keats's death, Shelley wrote and published a poem which was always sub-titled as an elegy for him – 'Adonais'; one of the greatest and at the same time one of the most typical Romantic poems, Romantic in its aspirations, its language, its sense of the sublime importance of the poet. These are its four concluding stanzas:

from Adonais

The One remains, the many change and pass;
Heaven's light for ever shines, Earth's shadows fly;
Life, like a dome of many-coloured glass,
Stains the white radiance of Eternity,

Until Death tramples it to fragments. – Die,
If thou wouldst be with that which thou dost seek!
Follow where all is fled! – Rome's azure sky,
Flowers, ruins, statues, music, words, are weak
The glory they transfuse with fitting truth to speak.

Why linger, why turn back, why shrink, my Heart?
Thy hopes are gone before: from all things here
They have departed; thou shouldst now depart!
A light is passed from the revolving year,
And man, and woman; and what still is dear
Attracts to crush, repels to make thee wither.
The soft sky smiles, the low wind whispers near:
'Tis Adonais calls! oh, hasten thither,
No more let Life divide what Death can join together.

That Light whose smile kindles the Universe,
That Beauty in which all things work and move,
That Benediction which the eclipsing Curse
Of birth can quench not, that sustaining Love
Which through the web of being blindly wove
By man and beast and earth and air and sea,
Burns bright or dim, as each are mirrors of
The fire for which all thirst; now beams on me
Consuming the last clouds of cold mortality.

The breath whose might I have invoked in song
Descends on me; my spirit's bark is driven
Far from the shore, far from the trembling throng
Whose sails were never to the tempest given;
The massy earth and sphered skies are riven!
I am borne darkly, fearfully, afar;
Whilst burning through the inmost veil of Heaven,
The soul of Adonais, like a star,
Beacons from the abode where the Eternal are.

Shelley himself was drowned off the coast of Italy in the year following Keats's death in Rome, in a way that almost appears to be prophesied in the final stanza of 'Adonais'. The names of Shelley and Keats, commemorated together in the Protestant Cemetery in Rome, have been linked ever since. Keats's handful of years of writing poetry seems almost a race with time, with his masterpieces concentrated into 1819 and 1820.

80. Keats's unusually wide reading provided much of the source material for his own poetry. The picture of Shakespeare in the background was given to Keats by his former landlady and he kept it until his death.

He was precocious, he had read amazingly widely, and a great deal of the nourishment for his own poems came from his reading. Myths and legends, Homer's ancient poems and Chaucer's medieval ones, the Romantic rediscovery of old ballads – all came together in the fusion of Keats's imagination. At the beginning of his most productive year, 1819, he wrote a mysterious, almost literally un-earthly ballad of his own – un-earthly, and yet full of precision:

La Belle Dame Sans Merci

'O what can ail thee, knight-at-arms,
Alone and palely loitering?
The sedge is wither'd from the lake,
And no birds sing.

'O what can ail thee, knight-at-arms,
So haggard and so woe-begone?
The squirrel's granary is full,
And the harvest's done.

'I see a lily on thy brow
With anguish moist and fever dew;
And on thy cheek a fading rose
Fast withereth too.'

'I met a lady in the meads,
Full beautiful – a faery's child,
Her hair was long, her foot was light,
And her eyes were wild.

'I made a garland for her head,
And bracelets too, and fragrant zone;
She look'd at me as she did love,
And made sweet moan.

'I set her on my pacing steed
And nothing else saw all day long,
For sideways would she lean and sing
A faery's song.

'She found me roots of relish sweet,
And honey wild and manna dew,
And sure in language strange she said,
"I love thee true!"

'She took me to her elfin grot,
And there she wept and sigh'd full sore;
And there I shut her wild, wild eyes
With kisses four.

'And there she lullèd me asleep,
And there I dream'd – Ah! woe betide!
The latest dream I ever dream'd
On the cold hill's side.

'I saw pale kings and princes too,
Pale warriors, death-pale were they all;
Who cried – "La belle Dame sans Merci
Hath thee in thrall!"

'I saw their starved lips in the gloam
With horrid warning gapèd wide,
And I awoke and found me here
On the cold hill's side.

'And this is why I sojourn here
Alone and palely loitering,
Though the sedge is wither'd from the lake,
And no birds sing.'

In the autumn of that same year, Keats was in Winchester, and he wrote from there to a friend:

How beautiful the season is now – how fine the air, a temperate sharpness about it . . . I never liked stubble fields so much as now – aye, better than the chilly green of the Spring. Somehow a stubble plain looks warm . . . This struck me so much in my Sunday's walk that I composed upon it.

A few days later, Keats sent to another friend the completed ode 'To Autumn': rhapsodical, sensuous, in a sense artificial, but at the same time deeply felt and richly powerful:

To Autumn

Season of mists and mellow fruitfulness,
Close bosom-friend of the maturing sun;
Conspiring with him how to load and bless
With fruit the vines that round the thatch-eaves run;
To bend with apples the moss'd cottage-trees,
And fill all fruit with ripeness to the core;
To swell the gourd, and plump the hazel shells
With a sweet kernel; to set budding more,
And still more, later flowers for the bees,
Until they think warm days will never cease,
For Summer has o'er-brimm'd their clammy cells.

Who hath not seen thee oft amid thy store?
Sometimes whoever seeks abroad may find
Thee sitting careless on a granary floor,
Thy hair soft-lifted by the winnowing wind;
Or on a half-reap'd furrow sound asleep,
Drows'd with the fume of poppies, while thy hook
Spares the next swath and all its twined flowers:

81. 'Season of mists and mellow fruitfulness,
    Close bosom-friend of the maturing sun . . .'

And sometimes like a gleaner thou dost keep
Steady thy laden head across a brook;
Or by a cyder-press, with patient look,
Thou watchest the last oozings hours by hours.

Where are the songs of Spring? Ay, where are they?
Think not of them, thou hast thy music too, –
While barred clouds bloom the soft-dying day,
And touch the stubble-plains with rosy hue;
Then in a wailful choir the small gnats mourn
Among the river sallows, borne aloft
Or sinking as the light wind lives or dies;
And full-grown lambs loud bleat from hilly bourne;
Hedge-crickets sing; and now with treble soft
The red-breast whistles from a garden-croft;
And gathering swallows twitter in the skies.

The sensuousness and ornateness of 'To Autumn' combine to make
something quite different from, say, Wordsworth's poems, which at their
best aim for naturalness and achieve it. Keats was a very conscious,
indeed very *self*-conscious artist; and yet, paradoxically, he keeps his own

self, the 'I' figure, out of his poems much more than Wordsworth does. His imagination aimed at what, in a letter, he called 'negative capability'.

A poet who flamboyantly and with great self-assurance constantly thrust his own personality, or range of personalities, into his work was George Gordon, Lord Byron. Witty, rakish, fearless, contemptuous of fools and dullards, sexually attractive, sexually predatory, aristocratic and capable of a deep and infectious melancholy too, Byron became a Romantic hero not only in England but throughout Europe; and not only a hero, but notorious too. That was part of the appeal, summed up in the old phrase about Byron being 'mad, bad, and dangerous to know'.

82. Lord Byron painted in 1813, looking the very image of the Romantic poet.

Before he was thirty, he was an extremely famous and best-selling poet, chiefly on the strength of *Childe Harold's Pilgrimage*; but few people today would argue that *Childe Harold* survives in the way that a slightly later long poem of Byron's does. One day, late in 1818, there arrived on the desk of

John Murray, his loyal publisher, the first two cantos of *Don Juan*, to be published (anonymously, though the name of the author was an open secret) the following July. The poem stretched to seventeen cantos in the end, and Byron took the final section with him to Greece in 1823. But he added nothing to it there and, when he died at Missolonghi the following year, on his expedition to help the Greeks in their war of independence against the Turks, it was still unfinished.

But *Don Juan* is Byron's masterpiece: a great comic poem which is also a great comic autobiography, full of the multitude of things that passed through Byron's fertile mind during the thirty-six crowded years of his life. Eight stanzas from Canto I – cynical, exuberant, sardonic, mocking and self-mocking – give some flavour of this endlessly entertaining Romantic fragmentary epic:

from Don Juan, Canto I

But now at thirty years my hair is grey
   (I wonder what it will be like at forty?
I thought of a peruke the other day);
   My heart is not much greener, and in short I
Have squandered my whole summer while 'twas May,
   And feel no more the spirit to retort. I
Have spent my life, both interest and principal,
And deem not, what I deemed, my soul invincible.

No more – no more – oh never more on me
   The freshness of the heart can fall like dew,
Which out of all the lovely things we see
   Extracts emotions beautiful and new,
Hived in our bosoms like the bag o' the bee.
   Think'st thou the honey with those objects grew?
Alas, 'twas not in them, but in thy power
To double even the sweetness of a flower.

No more – no more – oh never more, my heart,
   Canst thou be my sole world, my universe!
Once all in all, but now a thing apart,
   Thou canst not be my blessing or my curse.
The illusion's gone forever, and thou art
   Insensible, I trust, but none the worse,
And in thy stead I've got a deal of judgement,
Though heaven knows now it ever found a lodgement.

83. A cartoon of Byron at work in
Venice, wearing dressing-gown and
slippers, and urged on by the
Devil.

My days of love are over, me no more
   The charms of maid, wife, and still less of widow
Can make the fool of which they made before;
   In short, I must not lead the life I did do.
The credulous hope of mutual minds is o'er,
   The copious use of claret is forbid too,
So for a good old-gentlemanly vice,
I think I must take up with avarice.

Ambition was my idol, which was broken
　　Before the shrines of Sorrow and of Pleasure;
And the two last have left me many a token
　　O'er which reflection may be made at leisure.
Now, like Friar Bacon's brazen head, I've spoken,
'Time is, Time was, Time's past.' A chymic treasure
Is glittering youth, which I have spent betimes,
My heart in passion and my head on rhymes.

What is the end of fame? 'Tis but to fill
　　A certain portion of uncertain paper.
Some liken it to climbing up a hill,
　　Whose summit, like all hills, is lost in vapour.
For this men write, speak, preach, and heroes kill,
　　And bards burn what they call their midnight taper,
To have, when the original is dust,
A name, a wretched picture, and worse bust.

What are the hopes of man? Old Egypt's King
　　Cheops erected the first pyramid,
And largest, thinking it was just the thing
　　To keep his memory whole and mummy hid;
But somebody or other rummaging,
　　Burglariously broke his coffin's lid.
Let not a monument give you or me hopes,
Since not a pinch of dust remains of Cheops.

But I being fond of true philosophy
　　Say very often to myself, 'Alas!
All things that have been born were born to die,
　　And flesh (which Death mows down to hay) is grass.
You've passed your youth not so unpleasantly,
　　And if you had it o'er again, 'twould pass;
So thank your stars that matters are no worse
And read your Bible, sir, and mind your purse.'

TEN

Victorians
1837-1901

In 1837, when Victoria became Queen, she inherited as Poet Laureate a poet who by then seemed only slightly less ludicrous than his predecessor in the post, Henry James Pye. Robert Southey had been pouring out vast quantities of verse and prose for more years than most people could remember. The time had long gone by when Southey could be lumped in (as Byron had done) with Wordsworth and Coleridge as one of 'the Lakers': poets who were supposed to have turned the Lake District into a colony of the Muses. Poor Southey was a survivor, just, from the heady days of possible revolution and of such notions as 'Pantisocracy', whereby he and Coleridge and other selected souls were going to found a truly communist society on a river-bank in Georgia.

But in 1837 there were few other survivors. Coleridge was dead; Byron, Shelley and Keats were dead; Southey himself had worked so hard that he was suffering from what was called 'softening of the brain'. Wordsworth was still there, aged sixty-seven, and his brain wasn't soft at all: it was hard, resolute, testily reactionary and capable of producing verse after verse. So, when Southey died in 1843, Wordsworth became Laureate, with seven years left before his own death, and, it seemed, the last grand old man of British letters.

It may have seemed a dead period, or a blank period. But the new men, those we know as the Victorians, were there, with talent, ambition and a potential audience. In the year of Victoria's coronation, Alfred Tennyson was twenty-eight. The son of a Lincolnshire clergyman, he had elder brothers who were poets too. Together they had published a book of poems ten years earlier, when Alfred was only eighteen. But that book, and indeed another one, published by Alfred himself three years later, had attracted little attention. It was a two-volume collection of poems in 1842 that made a wide audience realise that a powerful new poet had arrived.

But Alfred himself was still suffering from the greatest emotional blow of his life: the death of his close friend Arthur Hallam. Both men were in their early twenties when Hallam died: they had been at Cambridge

84. When Queen Victoria was crowned in 1838 Coleridge, Byron, Shelley and Keats were all dead; Wordsworth was aged 68 and still writing verse; Tennyson was 28 and not yet famous. A new era was to begin, in literature as in history.

together, and what had grown between them was what a later, more
prurient, age might call homosexual love – totally unphysical, but highly
emotional in its devotion. Within a few weeks of Hallam's death,
Tennyson began to write an elegiac poem which was to occupy him on
and off for the next dozen or fifteen years: 'In Memoriam'. This slowly
assembled elegy, not published until 1850, is, quite naturally, long: over
130 sections of varying lengths, though each stanza is assembled in
exactly the same four-line form. There follow five sections from what
Tennyson many years later called 'rather the cry of the whole human race
than mine':

85. Alfred Tennyson
shortly before
publication of the book
that was to make his
name.

from In Memoriam

Dark house, by which once more I stand
Here in the long unlovely street,
Doors, where my heart was used to beat
So quickly, waiting for a hand,

A hand that can be clasped no more –
Behold me, for I cannot sleep,
And like a guilty thing I creep
At earliest morning to the door.

He is not here; but far away
The noise of life begins again,
And ghastly through the drizzling rain
On the bald street breaks the blank day.

*   *   *

The path by which we twain did go,
Which led by tracts that pleased us well,
Through four sweet years arose and fell,
From flower to flower, from snow to snow:

And we with singing cheered the way,
And, crowned with all the season lent,
From April on to April went,
And glad at heart from May to May:

But where the path we walked began
To slant the fifth autumnal slope,
As we descended following Hope,
There sat the Shadow feared of man;

Who broke our fair companionship,
And spread his mantle dark and cold,
And wrapt thee formless in the fold,
And dulled the murmur on thy lip,

And bore thee where I could not see
Nor follow, though I walk in haste,
And think, that somewhere in the waste
The Shadow sits and waits for me.

*   *   *

86. Tennyson as a student at Cambridge, sketched by his friend James Spedding.

Be near me when my light is low,
When the blood creeps, and the nerves prick
And tingle; and the heart is sick,
And all the wheels of Being slow.

Be near me when the sensuous frame
Is wrecked with pangs that conquer trust:
And Time, a maniac scattering dust,
And Life, a Funy slinging flame.

Be near me when my faith is dry,
And men the flies of latter spring,
That lay their eggs, and sting and sing
And weave their petty cells and die.

87. (above) Arthur Hallam, Tennyson's close friend, also sketched by Spedding.

88. (below) A manuscript page of 'In Memoriam', the great elegiac poem which mourns Hallam's early death.

Be near me when I fade away,
To point the term of human strife,
And on the low dark verge of life
The twilight of eternal day.

* * *

Unwatched, the garden bough shall sway,
The tender blossom flutter down,
Unloved, that beech will gather brown,
This maple burn itself away;

Unloved, the sun-flower, shining fair,
Ray round with flames her disk of seed,
And many a rose-carnation feed
With summer spice the humming air;

Unloved, by many a sandy bar,
The brook shall babble down the plain,
At noon or when the lesser wain
Is twisting round the polar star;

Uncared for, gird the windy grove,
And flood the haunts of hern and crake;
Or into silver arrows break
The sailing moon in creek and cove;

Till from the garden and the wild
A fresh association blow,
And year by year the landscape grow
Familiar to the stranger's child;

As year by year the labourer tills
His wonted glebe, or lops the glades:
And year by year our memory fades
From all the circle of the hills.

* * *

Doors, where my heart was used to beat
So quickly, not as one that weeps
I come once more: the city sleeps;
I smell the meadow in the street;

I hear a chirp of birds; I see
Betwixt the black fronts long-withdrawn
A light-blue lane of early dawn,
And think of early days and thee,

And bless thee, for thy lips are bland,
And bright the friendship of thine eye;
And in my thoughts with scarce a sigh
I take the pressure of thine hand.

The Victorian age was a great age of elegies, of poems of death, and love, and death in love. It was also the first period in our history in which women took a significant and important place as poets. The wife of Robert Browning, Elizabeth Barrett Browning, was better known and had a higher reputation than he did for some years: her verse-novel, *Aurora Leigh*, was one of the great successes of the mid-century. The three Brontë sisters, Charlotte, Emily and Anne, all wrote poems as well as

89. Emily Brontë painted c. 1833 by her brother Branwell.

novels. Many of their poems were written almost as exercises, as part of
the imaginary kingdom called 'Gondal' which they invented along with
their brother Branwell. In Emily Brontë's poem 'The Visionary', one feels
the same strange and secret powers of her *Wuthering Heights* – wind,
snow, an isolated house, something imminent and inexplicable outside,
beyond the lamp and the window . . . :

The Visionary

Silent is the house: all are laid asleep:
One alone looks out o'er the snow-wreaths deep,
Watching every cloud, dreading every breeze
That whirls the wildering drift, and bends the groaning
    trees.

Cheerful is the hearth, soft the matted floor;
Not one shivering gust creeps through pane or door;
The little lamp burns straight, its rays shoot strong and
    far:
I trim it well, to be the wanderer's guiding-star.

Frown, my haughty sire! chide, my angry dame;
Set your slaves to spy; threaten me with shame:
But neither sire nor dame, nor prying serf shall know,
What angel nightly tracks that waste of frozen snow.

What I love shall come like visitant of air,
Safe in secret power from lurking human snare;
Who loves me, no word of mine shall e'er betray,
Though for faith unstained my life must forfeit pay.

Burn, then, little lamp; glimmer straight and clear –
Hush! a rustling wing stirs, methinks, the air:
He for whom I wait, thus ever comes to me;
Strange Power! I trust thy might; trust thou my
    constancy.

The Victorians were the great literary entertainers, tellers of
spellbinding tales and singers of songs. This was the age of Dickens and
Mendelssohn, and of a new large audience for literature and music, a
much larger cultivated class than had ever existed before. Tennyson was
part of all this: a man who gave a willing audience a wide variety of what
they wanted – stories (*The Idylls of the King*), sentiment (*Maud*), patriotism

('The Charge of the Light Brigade') and sheer musical pleasure, as in the lyrics from *The Princess*, such as 'Tears, idle tears', 'The splendour falls on castle walls', 'Sweet and low', and 'Now sleeps the crimson petal, now the white':

from The Princess

Now sleeps the crimson petal, now the white;
Nor waves the cypress in the palace walk;
Nor winks the gold fin in the porphyry font:
The fire-fly wakens: waken thou with me.

Now droops the milkwhite peacock like a ghost,
And like a ghost she glimmers on to me.

Now lies the Earth all Danae to the stars,
And all thy heart lies open unto me.

Now slides the silent meteor on, and leaves
A shining furrow, as thy thoughts in me.

Now folds the lily all her sweetness up,
And slips into the bosom of the lake:
So fold thyself, my dearest, thou, and slip
Into my bosom and be lost in me.

Like many poets before and since, Tennyson found inspiration in legends and characters from the remote past – from the stories of King Arthur and his knights in his *Idylls of the King*, and from the heroic epics of Homer's *Iliad* and *Odyssey*. In the monologue 'Ulysses', Tennyson imagines Ulysses towards the end of his life, back in Ithaca after his long wanderings and now restless to set out again. Tennyson said of the poem that he wrote it soon after Arthur Hallam's death, with a sense of loss and that all had gone by 'but that still life must be fought out to the end . . .':

Ulysses

It little profits that an idle king,
By this still hearth, among these barren crags,
Match'd with an agèd wife, I mete and dole
Unequal laws unto a savage race,
That hoard, and sleep, and feed, and know not me.

90. Tennyson photographed at the age of 55, when he had already been Poet Laureate for 14 years.

I cannot rest from travel: I will drink
Life to the lees: all times I have enjoy'd
Greatly, have suffer'd greatly, both with those
That loved me, and alone; on shore, and when
Thro' scudding drifts the rainy Hyades
Vext the dim sea: I am become a name;
For always roaming with a hungry heart
Much have I seen and known; cities of men
And manners, climates, councils, governments,
Myself not least, but honour'd of them all;
And drunk delight of battle with my peers,
Far on the ringing plains of windy Troy.
I am a part of all that I have met;
Yet all experience is an arch wherethro'
Gleams that untravell'd world, whose margin fades
For ever and for ever when I move.
How dull it is to pause, to make an end,
To rust unburnish'd, not to shine in use!

As tho' to breathe were life. Life piled on life
Were all too little, and of one to me
Little remains: but every hour is saved
From that eternal silence, something more,
A bringer of new things; and vile it were
For some three suns to store and hoard myself,
And this gray spirit yearning in desire
To follow knowledge like a sinking star,
Beyond the utmost bound of human thought.
This is my son, mine own Telemachus,
To whom I leave the sceptre and the isle –
Well-loved of me, discerning to fulfil
This labour, by slow prudence to make mild
A rugged people, and thro' soft degrees
Subdue them to the useful and the good.
Most blameless is he, centred in the sphere
Of common duties, decent not to fail
In offices of tenderness, and pay
Meet adoration to my household gods,
When I am gone. He works his work, I mine.
There lies the port; the vessel puffs her sail:
There gloom the dark broad seas. My mariners,
Souls that have toil'd, and wrought, and thought with me –
That ever with a frolic welcome took
The thunder and the sunshine, and opposed
Free hearts, free foreheads – you and I are old;
Old age hath yet his honour and his toil;
Death closes all: but something ere the end,
Some work of noble note, may yet be done,
Not unbecoming men that strove with Gods.
The lights begin to twinkle from the rocks:
The long day wanes: the slow moon climbs: the deep
Moans round with many voices. Come, my friends,
'Tis not too late to seek a newer world.
Push off, and sitting well in order smite
The sounding furrows; for my purpose holds
To sail beyond the sunset, and the baths
Of all the western stars, until I die.
It may be that the gulfs will wash us down:
It may be we shall touch the Happy Isles,
And see the great Achilles, whom we knew.
Tho' much is taken, much abides; and tho'
We are not now that strength which in old days
Moved earth and heaven; that which we are, we are;

One equal temper of heroic hearts,
Made weak by time and fate, but strong in will
To strive, to seek, to find, and not to yield.

Robert Browning, who along with Tennyson dominated the Victorian age, was wide-ranging too. He was another story-teller, often (as in his novel-length poem *The Ring and the Book*) even more copious than Tennyson. But his best poems of this kind are like strangely

91. Robert Browning. He has written in the bottom left-hand corner, 'This portrait was executed in Rome, in 1859, as a companion to that of E.B.B. . . .'

self-contained incidents from some lost play: a moment of reflection or self-revelation from which we, the audience, have to grasp what surrounds it. Many of these 'dramatic monologues' come from his book *Men and Women*, published in 1855, though Browning began them several years earlier and went on writing them for the rest of his life. One of them

is 'My Last Duchess'. In it, an Italian Renaissance princeling is showing a painting of his late wife to some representative of his prospective new wife's family. Immediately we are plunged into the snobbish and unscrupulous manoeuvring of this odious man – a speaking likeness from the past come to life:

My Last Duchess

That's my last Duchess painted on the wall,
Looking as if she were alive. I call
That piece a wonder, now: Fra Pandolf's hands
Worked busily a day, and there she stands.
Will't please you sit and look at her? I said
'Fra Pandolf' by design, for never read
Strangers like you that pictured countenance,
The depth and passion of its earnest glance,

But to myself they turned (since none puts by
The curtain I have drawn for you, but I)
And seemed as they would ask me, if they durst,
How such a glance came there; so, not the first
Are you to turn and ask thus. Sir, 'twas not
Her husband's presence only, called that spot
Of joy into the Duchess' cheek: perhaps
Fra Pandolf chanced to say 'Her mantle laps
Over my lady's wrist too much,' or 'Paint
Must never hope to reproduce the faint
Half-flush that dies along her throat': such stuff
Was courtesy, she thought, and cause enough
For calling up that spot of joy. She had
A heart – how shall I say? – too soon made glad,
Too easily impressed; she liked whate'er
She looked on, and her looks went everywhere.
Sir, 'twas all one! My favour at her breast,
The dropping of the daylight in the West,
The bough of cherries some officious fool
Broke in the orchard for her, the white mule
She rode with round the terrace – all and each
Would draw from her alike the approving speech,
Or blush, at least. She thanked men, – good! but
    thanked
Somehow – I know not how – as if she ranked
My gift of a nine-hundred-years-old name
With anybody's gift. Who'd stoop to blame
This sort of trifling? Even had you skill
In speech – (which I have not) – to make your will
Quite clear to such an one, and say, 'Just this
Or that in you disgusts me; here you miss,
Or there exceed the mark' – and if she let
Herself be lessened so, nor plainly set
Her wits to yours, forsooth, and made excuse,
– E'en then would be some stooping; and I choose
Never to stoop. Oh sir, she smiled, no doubt,
Much the same smile? This grew; I gave commands;
Then all smiles stopped together. There she stands
As if alive. Will't please you rise? We'll meet
The company below, then. I repeat,
The Count your master's known munificence
Is ample warrant that no just pretence
Of mine for dowry will be disallowed;
Though his fair daughter's self, as I avowed

> At starting, is my object. Nay, we'll go
> Together down, sir. Notice Neptune, though,
> Taming a sea-horse, thought a rarity,
> Which Claus of Innsbruck cast in bronze for me!

Browning, like Tennyson, could work on a much smaller scale. In his poem 'Meeting at Night', he catches in only twelve lines a deliciously surreptitious moment in a love affair. There is no need to know who the speaker is, or anything about whoever he is meeting – the urgency and ecstasy and excitement are all there:

Meeting at Night

> The grey sea and the long black land;
> And the yellow half-moon large and low;
> And the startled little waves that leap
> In fiery ringlets from their sleep,
> As I gain the cove with pushing prow,
> And quench its speed i' the slushy sand.
>
> Then a mile of warm sea-scented beach;
> Three fields to cross till a farm appears;
> A tap at the pane, the quick sharp scratch
> And blue spurt of a lighted match,
> And a voice less loud, thro' its joys and fears,
> Than the two hearts beating each to each!

In such poems as these, Browning has great confidence; and confidence can be seen as a mark of many of the early and mid-Victorian poets. But as the century went on (with, for example, Darwin's controversial theories about evolution taking hold), doubt began to erode religious faith, and we find a new, troubled Romanticism, not convinced by the old orthodoxies but unsure of the individual and of individual passions too.

Here one of the poets we particularly turn to is Matthew Arnold. Arnold was a product of the high-minded, duty-ridden early Victorian intellectual aristocracy (his father was Thomas Arnold, headmaster of Rugby and of *Tom Brown's Schooldays*), dissatisfied with the bland Anglicanism of his day but unable to find any firm substitute for it. Matthew Arnold confronted this loss directly in his key poem 'Dover Beach'. Here the setting, the descriptiveness, the glance back towards classical Greece, the sombre moralising, all blend together with great authority:

93. Matthew Arnold's
melancholy and
brooding air has been
captured in this
portrait by George
Watts.

Dover Beach

The sea is calm to-night.
The tide is full, the moon lies fair
Upon the Straits – on the French coast, the light
Gleams, and is gone; the cliffs of England stand,
Glimmering and vast, out in the tranquil bay.

Come to the window, sweet is the night air!
Only, from the long line of spray
Where the sea meets the moon-blanched sand,
Listen! you hear the grating roar
Of pebbles which the waves suck back, and fling,
At their return, up the high strand,
Begin, and cease, and then again begin,
With tremulous cadence slow, and bring
The eternal note of sadness in.

Sophocles long ago
Heard it on the Aegean, and it brought
Into his mind the turbid ebb and flow,
Of human misery; we
Find also in the sound a thought,
Hearing it by this distant northern sea.

The sea of faith
Was once, too, at the full, and round earth's shore
Lay like the folds of a bright girdle furled;
But now I only hear
Its melancholy, long, withdrawing roar,
Retreating to the breath
Of the night-wind down the vast edges drear
And naked shingles of the world.

Ah, love, let us be true
To one another! for the world, which seems
To lie before us like a land of dreams,
So various, so beautiful, so new,
Hath really neither joy, nor love, nor light,
Nor certitude, nor peace, nor help for pain;
And we are here as on a darkling plain
Swept with confused alarms of struggle and flight,
Where ignorant armies clash by night.

CHRISTINA ROSSETTI
del. SEPTEMBER 1866

94. Christina Rossetti drawn by her brother.

Christina Rossetti, later in the century, was also part of a remarkable literary family. She was the sister of Dante Gabriel Rossetti, one of the founders of that group of painters and writers known as the Pre-Raphaelite Brotherhood. Many of her poems of elegiac devotion, lost love and regret, may be as much part of the passionate imagination as Emily Brontë's poems; but we do well not to confuse authenticity with documentary, or to see all emotion as tending towards what is nowadays called 'confessional poetry'. Does it really matter to whom this poem is addressed, or whether it was addressed to a 'real' person at all?

95. 'When I am dead, my dearest,
    Sing no sad songs for me . . .'

Song

When I am dead, my dearest,
Sing no sad songs for me;
Plant thou no roses at my head,
Nor shady cypress tree:
Be the green grass above me
With showers and dewdrops wet;
And if thou wilt, remember,
And if thou wilt, forget.

I shall not see the shadows,
I shall not feel the rain;
I shall not hear the nightingale
Sing on, as if in pain;
And dreaming through the twilight
That doth not rise nor set,
Haply I may remember,
And haply may forget.

To some people (to some of the Pre-Raphaelites, for example, such as Dante Gabriel Rossetti) Art and created Beauty could seem a substitute for lost religious faith: Art itself could sometimes seem a religion. Later in the nineteenth century there was to be the catch-phrase 'Art for Art's sake'. Christina Rossetti's brother, Dante Gabriel, was primarily a painter, whose paintings are full of colour, picturesqueness and sometimes mystery. The same qualities, touched with morbidity, can be found in his poems. The best of them is an unfinished visionary piece about death, 'The Orchard Pit':

The Orchard Pit

Piled deep below the screening apple-branch
   They lie with bitter apples in their hands:
And some are only ancient bones that blanch,
And some had ships that last year's wind did launch,
   And some were yesterday the lords of lands.

96. A self-portrait by Dante Gabriel Rossetti at the age of 19.

In the soft dell, among the apple-trees,
   High up above the hidden pit she stands,
And there for ever sings, who gave to these,
That lie below, her magic hour of ease,
   And those her apples holden in their hands.

This in my dreams is shown me; and her hair
   Crosses my lips and draws my burning breath;
Her song spreads golden wings upon the air,
Life's eyes are gleaming from her forehead fair,
   And from her breasts the ravishing eyes of Death.

Men say to me that sleep hath many dreams,
   Yet I knew never but this dream alone:
There, from a dried-up channel, once the stream's,
The glen slopes up; even such in sleep it seems
   As to my waking sight the place well known.

My love I call her, and she loves me well:
   But I love her as in the maelstrom's cup
The whirled stone loves the leaf inseparable
That clings to it round all the circling swell,
   And that the same last eddy swallows up.

When Tennyson died in 1892 and the question of who was to be the next Poet Laureate was being canvassed, Queen Victoria is reported to have said: 'I hear that Mr Swinburne is the best poet in my dominions'. Algernon Charles Swinburne did not in fact get the job (eventually it went to a very minor and rather ridiculous Tory journalist called Alfred Austin); but Swinburne was certainly wildly popular, particularly for his poems of the 1860s and particularly among the young intellectuals, students at Oxford and Cambridge, who loved him partly for his sexual and religious unorthodoxy (which is probably why he was not given the Laureateship) but chiefly for his hypnotically beautiful rhythms, saying mysterious and almost unparaphrasable things in wholly seductive ways – as in 'The Garden of Proserpine', from which these stanzas are taken:

97. Swinburne
portrayed by D. G.
Rossetti in 1861, a few
years before he
became successful and
popular.

from The Garden of Proserpine

Here, where the world is quiet;
Here, where all trouble seems
Dead winds' and spent waves' riot
In doubtful dreams of dreams;
I watch the green field growing
For reaping folk and sowing
For harvest-time and mowing,
A sleepy world of streams.

I am tired of tears and laughter,
And men that laugh and weep;
Of what may come hereafter
For men that sow to reap:
I am weary of days and hours,
Blown buds of barren flowers,
Desires and dreams and powers
And everything but sleep.

Pale, beyond porch and portal,
Crowned with calm leaves, she stands
Who gathers all things mortal
With cold immortal hands;
Her languid lips are sweeter
Than love's who fears to greet her
To men that mix and meet her
From many times and lands.

From too much love of living,
From hope and fear set free,
We thank with brief thanksgiving
Whatever gods may be
That no life lives for ever;
That dead men rise up never;
That even the weariest river
Winds somewhere safe to sea.

Then star nor sun shall waken,
Nor any change of light:
Nor sound of waters shaken,
Nor any sound or sight;
Nor wintry leaves nor vernal,
Nor days nor things diurnal;
Only the sleep eternal
In an eternal night.

98. A daguerrotype of Edgar Allan Poe
taken in November 1848, the month in which
he made an unsuccessful suicide attempt.

ELEVEN

American Pioneers
1849 - 1910

It took eighty years after the American Declaration of Independence in 1776 for a consciously American voice to break through: the voice of Walt Whitman, sounding (as he put it) his 'barbaric yawp over the roofs of the world'. Whitman's publication at his own expense of *Leaves of Grass* in 1855 decisively marks a moment not only of self-confidence but of separateness. Europe in general and England in particular were no longer to be the sole sources of culture.

Throughout the nineteenth century a number of American poets sold their books in Britain in respectable quantities: Bryant, Whittier, Emerson, above all Longfellow. But though all of them sometimes wrote consciously – often self-consciously – on American themes (such as Longfellow's historical narratives of *The Courtship of Miles Standish*, *Evangeline* and *Hiawatha*), all of them sounded basically *English* – which is why the English took to them. Whitman was different; and so, for rather separate reasons, was Edgar Allan Poe.

Poe had spent part of his orphaned childhood miserably in London between 1816 and 1820. He had unfulfilled ambitions not only to be a poet and fiction writer, which he was, but to be a powerful and influential man of letters. He was a fierce critic of what he saw as the mediocrity and imitativeness of practically all American poetry. What Poe looked for was not something specifically American like Whitman (and in any case *Leaves of Grass* was not published until over five years after Poe's death – Poe had never heard of Whitman): he looked for a new professionalism, a sense of dedication to Art which Poe, a Southerner, found lacking in the cosy, do-gooding atmosphere of the New England establishment of Longfellow and the others. Poe, in his poems as in his stories, tended towards fantasy and towards a sort of deliberate musicality. 'The City in the Sea' is a good example:

The City in the Sea

Lo! Death has reared himself a throne
In a strange city lying alone
Far down within the dim West,
Where the good and the bad and the worst and the best
Have gone to their eternal rest.
There shrines and palaces and towers
(Time-eaten towers that tremble not!)
Resemble nothing that is ours.
Around, by lifting winds forgot,
Resignedly beneath the sky
The melancholy waters lie.

No rays from the holy heaven come down
On the long night-time of that town;
But light from out the lurid sea
Streams up the turrets silently –
Gleams up the pinnacles far and free –
Up domes – up spires – up kingly halls –
Up fanes – up Babylon-like walls –
Up shadowy long-forgotten bowers
Of sculptured ivy and stone flowers –
Up many and many a marvellous shrine
Whose wreathèd friezes intertwine
The viol, the violet, and the vine.

Resignedly beneath the sky
The melancholy waters lie.
So blend the turrets and shadows there
That all seem pendulous in air,
While from a proud tower in the town
Death looks gigantically down.

There open fanes and gaping graves
Yawn level with the luminous waves;
But not the riches there that lie
In each idol's diamond eye –
Not the gaily-jewelled dead
Tempt the waters from their bed;
For no ripples curl, alas!
Along that wilderness of glass –
No swellings tell that winds may be
Upon some far-off happier sea –

No heavings hint that winds have been
On seas less hideously serene.

But lo, a stir is in the air!
The wave – there is a movement there!
As if the towers had thrust aside,
In slightly sinking, the dull tide –
As if their tops had feebly given
A void within the filmy Heaven.

The waves have now a redder glow –
The hours are breathing faint and low –
And when, amid no earthly moans,
Down, down that town shall settle hence,
Hell, rising from a thousand thrones,
Shall do it reverence.

After his death in 1849 Poe's reputation quite quickly spread, but as a poet much more into continental Europe, and particularly France, rather than England. Baudelaire and the French Symbolistes were deeply influenced by him. But it was Walt Whitman who, after the initial shock at his brash manner, his alleged formlessness and what was thought to be his too explicit sexuality, became truly international. His exuberance, his insolent bravado, the sheer intoxication of his life-force, made him a master:

from Song of Myself

Walt Whitman, a kosmos, of Manhattan the son,
Turbulent, fleshy, sensual, eating, drinking and
    breeding,
No sentimentalist, no stander above men and women or
    apart from them,
No more modest than immodest.

Unscrew the locks from the doors!
Unscrew the doors themselves from their jambs!

Whoever degrades another degrades me,
And whatever is done or said returns at last to me.

Through me the afflatus surging and surging, through
    me the current and index.

I speak the pass-word primeval, I give the sign of
    democracy,
By God! I will accept nothing which all cannot have
    their counterpart of on the same terms.

Through me many long dumb voices,
Voices of the interminable generations of prisoners and
    slaves,
Voices of the diseas'd and despairing and of thieves and
    dwarfs,
Voices of cycles of preparation and accretion,
And of the threads that connect the stars, and of wombs
    and of the father-stuff,
And of the rights of them the others are down upon,
Of the deform'd, trivial, flat, foolish, despised,
Fog in the air, beetles rolling balls of dung.

Through me forbidden voices,
Voices of sexes and lusts, voices veil'd and I remove the
    veil,
Voices indecent by me clarified and transfigur'd.

I do not press my fingers across my mouth,
I keep as delicate around the bowels as around the head
    and heart,
Copulation is no more rank to me than death is.

I believe in the flesh and the appetites,
Seeing, hearing, feeling, are miracles, and each part and
    tag of me is a miracle.

Divine am I inside and out, and I make holy whatever I
    touch or am touch'd from,
The scent of these arm-pits aroma finer than prayer,
This head more than churches, bibles, and all the
    creeds.

If I worship one thing more than another it shall be the
    spread of my own body, or any part of it,
Translucent mould of me it shall be you!
Shaded ledges and rests it shall be you!
Firm masculine colter it shall be you!
Whatever goes to the tilth of me it shall be you!

99. Walt Whitman
aged 36 in 1855, the
year he published
Leaves of Grass.

You my rich blood! your milky stream pale strippings of
   my life!
Breast that presses against other breasts it shall be you!
My brain it shall be your occult convolutions!
Root of wash'd sweet-flag! timorous pond-snipe! nest of
   guarded duplicate eggs! it shall be you!
Mix'd tussled hay of head, beard, brawn, it shall be you!
Trickling sap of maple, fibre of manly wheat, it shall be
   you!
Sun so generous it shall be you!
Vapors lighting and shading my face it shall be you!
You sweaty brooks and dews it shall be you!
Winds whose soft-tickling genitals rub against me it shall
   be you!
Broad muscular fields, branches of live oak, loving
   lounger in my winding paths, it shall be you!
Hands I have taken, face I have kiss'd, mortal I have
   ever touch'd, it shall be you.

I dote on myself, there is that lot of me and all so
   luscious,
Each moment and whatever happens thrills me with joy,

I cannot tell how my ankles bend, nor whence the cause
    of my faintest wish,
Nor the cause of the friendship I emit, nor the cause of
    the friendship I take again.

That I walk up my stoop, I pause to consider if it really
    be,
A morning-glory at my windows satisfies me more than
    the metaphysics of books.

To behold the day-break!
The little light fades the immense and diaphanous
    shadows,
The air tastes good to my palate.

Hefts of the moving world at innocent gambols silently
    rising freshly exuding,
Scooting obliquely high and low.

Something I cannot see puts upward libidinous prongs,
Seas of bright juice suffuse heaven.

The earth by the sky staid with, the daily close of their
    junction,
The heav'd challenge from the east that moment over
    my head,
The mocking taunt, See then whether you shall be
    master!

Whitman was a passionate admirer of Abraham Lincoln, and after Lincoln's assassination in 1865 he wrote a number of poems about him, most importantly a long sixteen-part elegy which begins with the lines:

When lilacs last in the dooryard bloom'd,
And the great star early droop'd in the western sky in
    the night,
I mourn'd, and yet shall mourn with ever-returning
    spring.

Ever-returning spring, trinity sure to me you bring,
Lilac blooming perennial and drooping star in the west,
And thought of him I love.

Here is part of that poem, a self-contained section to which Whitman
originally gave the sub-title 'Death Carol':

from When lilacs last in the dooryard bloom'd

Come lovely and soothing death,
Undulate round the world, serenely arriving, arriving,
In the day, in the night, to all, to each,
Sooner or later delicate death.

Prais'd be the fathomless universe,
For life and joy, and for objects and knowledge curious,
And for love, sweet love – but praise! praise! praise!
For the sure-enwinding arms of cool-enfolding death.

Dark mother always gliding near with soft feet,
Have none chanted for thee a chant of fullest welcome?
Then I chant it for thee, I glorify thee above all,
I bring thee a song that when thou must indeed come,
    come unfalteringly.

Approach strong deliveress,
When it is so, when thou hast taken them I joyously sing
    the dead,
Lost in the loving floating ocean of thee,
Laved in the flood of thy bliss O death.

From me to thee glad serenades,
Dances for thee I propose saluting thee, adornments and
    feastings for thee,
And the sights of the open landscape and the
    high-spread sky are fitting,
And life and the fields, and the huge and thoughtful
    night.

The night in silence under many a star,
The ocean shore and the husky whispering wave whose
    voice I know,
And the soul turning to thee O vast and well-veil'd
    death,
And the body gratefully nestling close to thee.

> Over the tree-tops I float thee a song,
> Over the rising and sinking waves, over the myriad fields
>   and the prairies wide,
> Over the dense-pack'd cities all and the teeming wharves
>   and ways,
> I float this carol with joy, with joy to thee O death.

But Whitman, for all the grandiose immensities of such poems, could and did work on a smaller scale too. His poem 'A Noiseless Patient Spider' is a very tender, yearning piece of concentration on something very small, a meditation on loneliness and isolation:

A Noiseless Patient Spider

> A noiseless patient spider,
> I mark'd where on a little promontory it stood isolated,
> Mark'd how to explore the vacant vast surrounding,
> It launch'd forth filament, filament, filament, out of
>   itself,
> Ever unreeling them, ever tirelessly speeding them.
>
> And you O my soul where you stand,
> Surrounded, detached, in measureless oceans of space,
> Ceaselessly musing, venturing, throwing, seeking the
>   spheres to connect them,
> Till the bridge you will need be form'd, till the ductile
>   anchor hold,
> Till the gossamer thread you fling catch somewhere, O
>   my soul.

The great trauma of mid-nineteenth century America was of course the Civil War, the War between the States. It broke out in 1861; and in the following year Julia Ward Howe published her 'Battle Hymn of the Republic'. The tune to which it became attached marks a slightly earlier stage in the struggle, and particularly the anti-slavery struggle – 'John Brown's Body'. It is an exalted, impassioned poem, totally assured that virtue and truth are on one side, and that God is behind them:

100. (above) Julia Ward Howe, author of several volumes of poetry, who became a prominent suffragette and the first woman member of the American Academy.

101. (below) General Grant (hatless, under the flag and eagle) and his Union generals, all together in one dramatic and romantic painting. 'The Battle Hymn of the Republic' was written for the Union forces.

The Battle Hymn of the Republic

Mine eyes have seen the glory of the coming of the Lord:
He is trampling out the vintage where the grapes of wrath are
    stored;
He hath loosed the fatal lightning of His terrible swift sword:
     His truth is marching on.

I have seen Him in the watch-fires of a hundred circling camps,
They have builded Him an altar in the evening dews and damps;
I can read His righteous sentence by the dim and flaring lamps:
     His day is marching on.

I have read a fiery gospel writ in burnished rows of steel:
'As ye deal with my contemners, so with you my grace shall deal;
Let the Hero, born of woman, crush the serpent with his heel,
     Since God is marching on.'

He has sounded forth the trumpet that shall never call retreat;
He is sifting out the hearts of men before His judgement seat:
Oh, be swift, my soul, to answer Him! Be jubilant, my feet!
     Our God is marching on.

In the beauty of the lilies Christ was born across the sea,
With a glory in his bosom that transfigures you and me:
As he died to make men holy, let us die to make men free,
     While God is marching on.

But the year in which Julia Ward Howe published that poem was also
the year of the Battle of Shiloh, one of the bloodiest battles of the war, in
which Grant's forces were routed by the Confederates. Like the Battle of
the Somme in 1916, Shiloh brought home for the first time to many
people the horrors of modern war; and in 1866, the year after the Civil
War ended, Herman Melville (already the author of that prose epic *Moby
Dick*) published a book of poems called *Battle Pieces*. In it is his 'Shiloh: a
Requiem'. If Julia Ward Howe's strident public hymn is one face of that
war, Melville's understated private poem is another, and equally valid:

102. (above) Herman
Melville wrote several
novels, including the
classic sea story *Moby
Dick*, but lack of
recognition made him
turn to writing poetry.
103. (below) The Battle
of Shiloh, in 1862, was
one of the bloodiest
battles of the
American Civil War.

Shiloh

A Requiem

Skimming lightly, wheeling still,
  The swallows fly low
Over the field in clouded days,
  The forest-field of Shiloh –
Over the field where April rain
Solaced the parched ones stretched in pain
Through the pause of night
That followed the Sunday fight
  Around the church of Shiloh –
The church so lone, the log-built one,
That echoed to many a parting groan
    And natural prayer
Of dying foemen mingled there –
Foemen at morn, but friends at eve –
  Fame or country least their care:
(What like a bullet can undeceive!)
  But now they lie low,
While over them the swallows skim,
  And all is hushed at Shiloh.

Saul Bellow has said that it was the 'great irrepressible solitaries' who set the tone of what was later to be seen as the nineteenth-century American experience – writers who for much of their lives worked in isolation, largely unrecognised, like Poe, Whitman and Melville. Of them all, none was more solitary than Emily Dickinson.

Emily Dickinson was born into a conventional, comfortable family in Amherst, Massachusetts, and spent almost the whole of her life there, from her birth in 1830 till her death in 1886. And she gradually withdrew, so that the family house was her whole geographical world: first the house and garden, then just the house, then simply and solely her room. Various explanations have been hazarded about why she did this – a hopeless love affair, some kind of breakdown – but whatever prompted the choice she made, the choice of solitude, it was an interior choice: her soul had chosen it – something touched on in several of her poems.

She had been writing poems since she was a girl; but suddenly, in her early thirties, she began to write as if possessed. She wrote 366 poems in 1862 alone. Only a handful were published during her lifetime, all of

104. The reclusive Emily Dickinson wrote intensely personal and often spiritual poetry, highly original in thought and form.

105. Emily Dickinson's bedroom, to which she
eventually withdrew and where she wrote in solitude.

them mangled by editors who thought they ought to be tidied up, or by
incompetent printers. For years these thousands of tiny poems lay in a box
in the family house in Amherst, and it was not until 1890, four years after
her death, that they began to be published. The full texts were not
published until 1955.

The characteristic Emily Dickinson tone is both immensely delicate
and immensely strong. She usually worked within a compass of twelve
lines or fewer: nothing could be more different from the irresistible
amplitude of Whitman. Her rhythms are shifting and subtle, but they are
almost all based on the simple verses of eighteenth-century hymns, the
hymns of the New England church. She turns them into sceptical riddles,
hard-edged and yet mysterious confrontations with Death and Immortal-
ity and Eternity. Slightly to alter what she says in one of them, Emily
Dickinson's poems are her 'letters to the world' – a world which ignores
her, and which she knows ignores her. There follow, in succession, five of
her miniature masterpieces:

This is my letter to the World
That never wrote to Me –
The simple News that Nature told –
With tender Majesty

Her Message is committed
To Hands I cannot see –
For love of Her – Sweet – countrymen –
Judge tenderly – of Me

*   *   *

I felt a Funeral, in my Brain,
And Mourners to and fro
Kept treading – treading – till it seemed
That Sense was breaking through –

And when they all were seated,
A Service, like a Drum –
Kept beating – beating – till I thought
My Mind was going numb –

And then I heard them lift a Box
And creak across my Soul
With those same Boots of Lead, again,
Then Space – began to toll,

As all the Heavens were a Bell,
And Being, but an Ear,
And I, and Silence, some strange Race
Wrecked, solitary, here –

And then a Plank in Reason, broke,
And I dropped down, and down –
And hit a World, at every plunge,
And Finished knowing – then –

*   *   *

I heard a Fly buzz – when I died –
The Stillness in the Room
Was like the Stillness in the Air –
Between the Heaves of Storm –

The Eyes around – had wrung them dry –
And Breaths were gathering firm
For that last Onset – when the King
Be witnessed – in the Room –

I willed my Keepsakes – Signed away
What portion of me be
Assignable – and then it was
There interposed a Fly –

With Blue – uncertain stumbling Buzz –
Between the light – and me –
And then the Windows failed – and then
I could not see to see –

                    *   *   *

Because I could not stop for Death –
He kindly stopped for me –
The Carriage held but just Ourselves –
And Immortality.

We slowly drove – He knew no haste
And I had put away
My labor and my leisure too,
For His Civility –

We passed the School, where Children strove
At Recess – in the Ring –
We passed the Fields of Gazing Grain –
We passed the Setting Sun –

Or rather – He passed Us –
The Dews drew quivering and chill –
For only Gossamer, my Gown –
My Tippet – only Tulle –

We paused before a House that seemed
A Swelling of the Ground –
The Roof was scarcely visible –
The Cornice – in the Ground –

Since then – 'tis Centuries – and yet
Feels shorter than the Day
I first surmised the Horses' Heads
Were toward Eternity –

*   *   *

My life closed twice before its close –
It yet remains to see
If Immortality unveil
A third event to me

So huge, so hopeless to conceive
As these that twice befell.
Parting is all we know of heaven,
And all we need of hell.

That theme of isolation, of disappointment, even of despair, in Emily
Dickinson is in a way as much a part of the American Dream as Walt
Whitman's confident optimism. Where there are great hopes, there are
also great disappointments. A more sardonic version of this can be found
in the poems of another solitary soul, Edwin Arlington Robinson. Though
unlike Emily Dickinson he eventually won considerable literary fame, and
even popularity – he was admired and praised by the President, Theodore
Roosevelt – Robinson was very much a loner, a mixture of nobility and
cynicism, brooding with classical precision on man's aspirations and
confusions. His imaginary portrait of the oddly named 'Miniver Cheevy'
is a kind of wry self-portrait too – a man who wanted to be anything but
himself and anywhere but here:

Miniver Cheevy

Miniver Cheevy, child of scorn,
    Grew lean while he assailed the seasons;
He wept that he was ever born,
    And he had reasons.

Miniver loved the days of old
    When swords were bright and steeds were prancing;
The vision of a warrior bold
    Would set him dancing.

Miniver sighed for what was not,
    And dreamed, and rested from his labors;
He dreamed of Thebes and Camelot,
    And Priam's neighbors.

106. Edwin Arlington Robinson drawn two years before his death in 1935.

Miniver mourned the ripe renown
  That made so many a name so fragrant;
He mourned Romance, now on the town,
  And Art, a vagrant.

Miniver loved the Medici,
  Albeit he had never seen one;
He would have sinned incessantly
  Could he have been one.

Miniver cursed the commonplace
  And eyed a khaki suit with loathing;
He missed the medieval grace
  Of iron clothing.

Miniver scorned the gold he sought,
  But sore annoyed was he without it;
Miniver thought, and thought, and thought,
  And thought about it.

Miniver Cheevy, born too late,
  Scratched his head and kept on thinking;
Miniver coughed, and called it fate,
  And kept on drinking.

TWELVE

Romantics and Realists
1870 - 1920

> Well, world, you have kept faith with me,
>   Kept faith with me;
> Upon the whole you have proved to be
>   Much as you said you were.
> Since as a child I used to lie
> Upon the leaze and watch the sky,
> Never, I own, expected I
>   That life would all be fair.

When Thomas Hardy wrote those words on his eighty-sixth birthday, the twentieth century was already well advanced. But the childhood at which Hardy looked back was part of the Victorian age, the age of Tennyson and Browning, and as far as Hardy himself was concerned a deeply rural childhood and young manhood, in an England that by the time he died in 1928 was almost unrecognisable. As a novelist, he had become the chronicler of Wessex – as much a country of the mind as a real place – and Wessex was the setting, too, of many of his poems, early and late.

107. An early photograph of Thomas Hardy, aged about 18.

Hardy had begun as a poet, and had then largely abandoned poetry as he became an industrious and successful novelist; but in the furore over the publication of *Jude the Obscure* in 1896 (the novel was thought by many to be blasphemously nihilistic), he returned to poetry, digging out and publishing many of the poems he had written in the 1860s. He continued to be a prolific writer of new poems almost until the day of his death.

From those poems of the 1860s, and from that Wessex, there is a sharply characteristic little encounter between the country and the city, between innocence and experience, between two kinds of morality, in Hardy's dialogue between two girls in 'The Ruined Maid':

The Ruined Maid

'O 'Melia, my dear, this does everything crown!
Who could have supposed I should meet you in Town?
And whence such fair garments, such prosperi-ty?' –
'O didn't you know I'd been ruined?' said she.

– 'You left us in tatters, without shoes or socks,
Tired of digging potatoes, and spudding up docks;
And now you've gay bracelets and bright feathers three!' –
'Yes: that's how we dress when we're ruined,' said she.

– 'At home in the barton you said "thee" and "thou,"
And "thik oon," and "theas oon," and "t'other"; but
    now
Your talking quite fits 'ee for high compa-ny!' –
'Some polish is gained with one's ruin,' said she.

– 'Your hands were like paws then, your face blue and
    bleak
But now I'm bewitched by your delicate cheek,
And your little gloves fit as on any la-dy!' –
'We never do work when we're ruined,' said she.

– 'You used to call home-life a hag-ridden dream,
And you'd sigh, and you'd sock; but at present you seem
To know not of megrims or melancho-ly!' –
'True. One's pretty lively when ruined,' said she.

– 'I wish I had feathers, a fine sweeping gown,
And a delicate face, and could strut about Town!' –
'My dear – a raw country girl, such as you be,
Cannot quite expect that. You ain't ruined,' said she.

The titles of some of Hardy's books of poems suggest much of his habitual subject matter: *Satires of Circumstance, Human Shows, Moments of Vision* – not 'moments of vision' in any religious sense (Hardy was a profound sceptic), but moments of seeing things as they really are – as in a short poem which beautifully catches a moment of chilling revelation, of human vanity and its ironies:

In Church

'And now to God the Father,' he ends,
And his voice thrills up to the topmost tiles:
Each listener chokes as he bows and bends,
And emotion pervades the crowded aisles.
Then the preacher glides to the vestry-door,
And shuts it, and thinks he is seen no more.

The door swings softly ajar meanwhile,
And a pupil of his in the Bible class,
Who adores him as one without gloss or guile,
Sees her idol stand with a satisfied smile
And re-enact at the vestry-glass
Each pulpit gesture in deft dumb-show
That had moved the congregation so.

Hardy's first wife, Emma, died in 1912. It had been in many ways a difficult marriage, but in the months following her death (and indeed for the rest of his life, even after his second marriage) Hardy was invaded by feelings of remorse, and by memories of earlier and happier days. In 1912 and 1913 he wrote a group of twenty or so poems which again and again go back and poignantly retrieve those memories. Among them is 'At Castle Boterel':

At Castle Boterel

As I drive to the junction of lane and highway,
And the drizzle bedrenches the waggonette,
I look behind at the fading byway,
And see on its slope, now glistening wet,
Distinctly yet

Myself and a girlish form benighted
In dry March weather. We climb the road
Beside a chaise. We had just alighted

To ease the sturdy pony's load
When he sighed and slowed.

What we did as we climbed, and what we talked of
Matters not much, nor to what it led, –
Something that life will not be balked of
Without rude reason till hope is dead,
And feeling fled.

It filled but a minute. But was there ever
A time of such quality, since or before,
In that hill's story? To one mind never,
Though it has been climbed, foot-swift, foot-sore,
By thousands more.

Primaeval rocks form the road's steep border,
And much have they faced there, first and last,
Of the transitory in Earth's long order;
But what they record in colour and cast
Is – that we two passed.

And to me, though Time's unflinching rigour,
In mindless rote, has ruled from sight
The substance now, one phantom figure
Remains on the slope, as when that night
Saw us alight.

I look and see it there, shrinking, shrinking,
I look back at it amid the rain
For the very last time; for my sand is sinking,
And I shall traverse old love's domain
Never again.

Hardy was a romantic and a realist. In the poems as in the novels, human beings are at the mercy of chance or circumstance or what looks like coincidence. There is the mystery of love, its exaltations and its obsessions; and there is the inexplicable advance of age, with its restrictions and humiliations. Hardy always seemed ready – and he knew it – to fall in love with beautiful women: but it was usually a love that toyed with his imagination rather than reality, a kind of sardonic idealism flirting with reticence. In just twelve lines, Hardy sees his middle-aged reflection in the mirror, and captures a moment of truth:

I Look into My Glass

I look into my glass,
And view my wasting skin,
And say, 'Would God it came to pass
My heart had shrunk as thin!'

For then, I, undistrest
By hearts grown cold to me,
Could lonely wait my endless rest
With equanimity.

But time, to make me grieve,
Part steals, lets part abide;
And shakes this fragile frame at eve
With throbbings of noontide.

So, thirty years later, beyond middle age and looking back with wry acceptance on all that had passed, he wrote what he called 'A Consideration' or 'A Reflection' on his eighty-sixth birthday. It was

108. Thomas Hardy painted by Strang two years before he died.

Hardy's address to the world after a lifetime in which, as the poem's title quizzically has it, 'He Never Expected Much':

He Never Expected Much

Well, World, you have kept faith with me,
　　　Kept faith with me;
Upon the whole you have proved to be
　　　Much as you said you were.
Since as a child I used to lie
Upon the leaze and watch the sky,
Never, I own, expected I
　　　That life would all be fair.

'Twas then you said, and since have said,
　　　Times since have said,
In that mysterious voice you shed
　　　From clouds and hills around:
'Many have loved me desperately,
Many with smooth serenity,
While some have shown contempt of me
　　　Till they dropped underground.

'I do not promise overmuch,
　　　Child; overmuch;
Just neutral-tinted haps and such,'
　　　You said to minds like mine.
Wise warning for your credit's sake!
Which I for one failed not to take,
And hence could stem such strain and ache
　　　As each year might assign.

An almost exact contemporary of Hardy's, but who died almost forty years before him, totally unknown as a poet in his lifetime except by a few close friends, was Gerard Manley Hopkins. Hopkins became a Roman Catholic convert while he was a young man at Oxford, and began his training as a Jesuit priest when he was twenty-four. He wrote poetry from an early age; but when he took on the discipline and dedication of his Jesuit novitiate, he felt that he had to put away all such distractions.

So there were seven years of deliberate drought, until a chance remark from his rector in his Jesuit college launched him into one of the finest and strangest religious poems in English, 'The Wreck of the *Deutschland*'. He

109. Gerard Manley Hopkins' ecstatic and visionary poetry was not published until thirty years after his death.

had, he said in a letter, 'long had haunting my ear the echo of a new rhythm which now I realised on paper'; and, having realised it once in 'The Wreck of the *Deutschland*', he found that he could use it again, and use it with justification, to the greater glory of God.

In 1877, one of his two most productive years, he wrote a dozen or so poems of celebration which are unique both in their visionary ecstasy and in the audacity of their language and rhythms. Hopkins's treatment of language was condensed, energetic, aiming for the particularity of words as his eyes aimed for the particularity of things – what he called the 'inscape' of things, those God-created minute characteristics which differentiate one thing from another. So, in his poem 'Pied Beauty', he exults in the dappled, the subtle, the special:

Pied Beauty

Glory be to God for dappled things –
For skies of couple-colour as a brinded cow;
For rose-moles all in stipple upon trout that swim;
Fresh fire-coal chestnut-falls; finches' wings;
Landscape plotted and pieced – fold, fallow, and plough;
And all trades, their gear and tackle and trim.

All things counter, original, spare, strange;
Whatever is fickle, freckled (who knows how?)
With swift, slow; sweet, sour; adazzle, dim;
He fathers-forth whose beauty is past change:
                    Praise him.

In that same year, 1877, Hopkins composed what at the time he called 'the best thing I ever wrote' – a hymn of wonder and joy at the sight of a falcon in the sky, and, through the falcon, a hymn of praise to God:

The Windhover

I caught this morning morning's minion, king-
        dom of daylight's dauphin, dapple-dawn-drawn Falcon,
        in his riding
    Of the rolling level underneath him steady air, and striding
High there, how he rung upon the rein of a wimpling wing
In his ecstasy! then off, off forth on swing,
    As a skate's heel sweeps smooth on a bow-bend: the hurl
        and gliding
Rebuffed the big wind. My heart in hiding
Stirred for a bird, – the achieve of, the mastery of the thing!

Brute beauty and valour and act, oh, air, pride, plume, here
    Buckle! AND the fire that breaks from thee then, a billion
Times told lovelier, more dangerous, O my chevalier!
No wonder of it: shéer plód makes plough down sillion
Shine, and blue-bleak embers, ah my dear,
    Fall, gall themselves, and gash gold-vermilion.

110. Survivors leaving the wrecked *Deutschland*, subject of one of the finest and strangest religious poems in English, written by Hopkins after a seven-year break from writing poetry.

But the emotion in Hopkins's poems does not simply reflect joy. There is loss, as there was loss in 'The Wreck of the *Deutschland*': loss at the decay of things, and loss of faith, too, in his own abilities and even in the power of God to save him from that loss. Sometimes he directed this sense of loss and sorrow outwards, as in the gently melancholy poem addressed (as he put it in a superscription) 'to a young child': a poem about the cycle of change and decay, 'Spring and Fall':

Spring and Fall

Márgarét, are you gríeving
Over Goldengrove unleaving?
Leáves, like the things of man, you
With your fresh thoughts care for, can you?
Áh ás the heart grows older
It will come to such sights colder
By and by, nor spare a sigh
Though worlds of wanwood leafmeal lie;
And yet you wíll weep and know why.
Now no matter, child, the name:
Sórrow's spríngs áre the same.
Nor mouth had, no nor mind, expressed
What heart heard of, ghost guessed:
It ís the blight man was born for,
It is Margaret you mourn for.

There was a bleaker, more personal, sense of loss in the eight so-called 'terrible sonnets' of the 1880s, in which the spirit is not one of celebration, as in 'Pied Beauty' and 'The Windhover', but of desolation, almost of despair. In 'I wake and feel the fell of dark', the images crowd in on one another – images of being smothered, isolated, soured, damned:

I wake and feel the fell of dark

I wake and feel the fell of dark, not day.
What hours, O what black hours we have spent
This night! what sights you, heart, saw; ways you went!
And more must, in yet longer light's delay.
　　With witness I speak this. But where I say
Hours I mean years, mean life. And my lament
Is cries countless, cries like dead letters sent
To dearest him that lives alas! away.

I am gall, I am heartburn. God's most deep decree
Bitter would have me taste: my taste was me;
Bones built in me, flesh filled, blood brimmed the curse.
　　Selfyeast of spirit a dull dough sours. I see
The lost are like this, and their scourge to be
As I am mine, their sweating selves; but worse.

The poems of Gerard Manley Hopkins were not collected and published until almost thirty years after his death; and even then they were slow to make much impact on a literary world that was not ready for them – they seemed too strange, and strangely mannered. But the poems of A. E. Housman had an immediate appeal, in spite of the fact that Housman was almost as reticent and withdrawn as Hopkins.

Housman's book *A Shropshire Lad* was published in 1896, and the Boer War soon afterwards helped to popularise Housman's mixture of patriotic pride and stoical gloom, of pessimism and nostalgia. On the face of it, his poems are very simple and very repetitive: they repeat again and again that love is fleeting, lovers fickle, youth decays into age, and that death is final. What makes them marvellous and memorable is no great profundity or originality of thought, but their seductive and instantly recognisable music, in which economy is mated with resonance. The two poems that follow come from the only other book apart from *A Shropshire Lad* which Housman published in his lifetime: he called the book, with a sense of finality, *Last Poems*. In both of them, what is celebrated is time passing. In both, despair is made beautiful:

111. A. E. Housman
was one of the most
widely read poets of
his time.

Tell me not here, it needs not saying,
    What tune the enchantress plays
In aftermaths of soft September
    Or under blanching mays,
For she and I were long acquainted
    And I knew all her ways.

On russet floors, by waters idle,
    The pine lets fall its cone;
The cuckoo shouts all day at nothing
    In leafy dells alone;
And traveller's joy beguiles in autumn
    Hearts that have lost their own.

On acres of the seeded grasses
    The changing burnish heaves;
Or marshalled under moons of harvest
    Stand still all night the sheaves;
Or beeches strip in storms for winter
    And stain the wind with leaves.

Possess, as I possessed a season,
    The countries I resign,
Where over elmy plains the highway
    Would mount the hills and shine,
And full of shade the pillared forest
    Would murmur and be mine.

For nature, heartless, witless nature,
    Will neither care nor know
What stranger's feet may find the meadow
    And trespass there and go,
Nor ask amid the dews of morning
    If they are mine or no.

          *   *   *

In valleys green and still
    Where lovers wander maying
They hear from over hill
    A music playing.

Behind the drum and fife,
    Past hawthornwood and hollow,
Through earth and out of life
    The soldiers follow.

The soldier's is the trade:
   In any wind or weather
He steals the heart of maid
   And man together.

The lover and his lass
   Beneath the hawthorn lying
Have heard the soldiers pass,
   And both are sighing.

And down the distance they
   With dying note and swelling
Walk the resounding way
   To the still dwelling.

Someone who knew 'the soldier's trade' rather closer to first-hand than Housman was Rudyard Kipling. He was not actually a soldier, but he was brought up in India and worked there as a journalist, and he knew very well the life of the British army in India, as well as the civil servants who ruled the country and the businessmen and landowners who exploited it.

From the beginning, as a young man, Kipling made India, or Anglo-India, his special province: it is not too much to say that, from an imaginative point of view, he created it for the world in his poems and stories, such as *Plain Tales from the Hills* and *Kim*. In 1886, at the age of

112. The British of the 1880s on an afternoon outing in 'the pleasant mountain-land' of Simla.

113. A wood engraving of Rudyard Kipling
made by William Nicholson.

twenty-one in Lahore, he published his book *Departmental Ditties*. It contains one particularly laconic, dry, sinister poem, in which the Old Testament story of King David's treatment of Uriah is put in an entirely Anglo-Indian context – 'The Story of Uriah':

114. The popular hill station Simla, c. 1900, where the British went each year to escape the worst of the heat.

The Story of Uriah

'Now there were two men in one city; the one rich, and the other poor.'

Jack Barrett went to Quetta
  Because they told him to.
He left his wife at Simla
  On three-fourths his monthly screw.
Jack Barrett died at Quetta
  Ere the next month's pay he drew.

Jack Barrett went to Quetta.
  He didn't understand
The reason of his transfer
  From the pleasant mountain-land.
The season was September,
  And it killed him out of hand.

Jack Barrett went to Quetta
    And there gave up the ghost,
Attempting two men's duty
    In that very healthy post;
And Mrs Barrett mourned for him
    Five lively months at most.

Jack Barrett's bones at Quetta
    Enjoy profound repose;
But I shouldn't be astonished
    If *now* his spirit knows
The reason of his transfer
    From the Himalayan snows.

And, when the Last Great Bugle Call
    Adown the Hurnai throbs,
And the last grim joke is entered
    In the big Black Book of Jobs,
And Quetta graveyards give again
    Their victims to the air,
I shouldn't like to be the man
    Who sent Jack Barrett there.

A few years later, Kipling published a whole book of poems concerned with the army, and particularly with the ordinary soldier: *Barrack-Room Ballads*. These poems are almost all written in a jaunty, strongly rhythmical Cockney, and many of them are convincing pieces of ventriloquism, seeming to be the voice itself of this army of mercenaries. The most chilling is about a military execution – 'Danny Deever':

Danny Deever

'What are the bugles blowin' for?' said Files-on-Parade.
'To turn you out, to turn you out,' the Colour-Sergeant said.
'What makes you look so white, so white?' said Files-on-Parade.
'I'm dreadin' what I've got to watch,' the Colour-Sergeant said.
    For they're hangin' Danny Deever, you can hear the Dead March
      play,
    The Regiment's in 'ollow square – they're hangin' him today;
    They've taken of his buttons off an' cut his stripes away,
    An' they're hangin' Danny Deever in the mornin'.

'What makes the rear-rank breathe so 'ard?' said Files-on-Parade.
'It's bitter cold, it's bitter cold,' the Colour-Sergeant said.
'What makes that front-rank man fall down?' said Files-on-Parade.
'A touch o' sun, a touch o' sun,' the Colour-Sergeant said.
   They're hangin' Danny Deever, they are marchin' of 'im round,
   They 'ave 'alted Danny Deever by 'is coffin on the ground;
   An' 'e'll swing in 'arf a minute for a sneakin' shootin' hound –
   O they're hangin' Danny Deever in the mornin'!

' 'Is cot was right-'and cot to mine,' said Files-on-Parade.
' 'E's sleepin' out an' far tonight,' the Colour-Sergeant said.
'I've drunk 'is beer a score o' times,' said Files-on-Parade.
' 'E's drinkin' bitter beer alone,' the Colour-Sergeant said.
   They are hangin' Danny Deever, you must mark 'im to 'is place,
   For 'e shot a comrade sleepin' – you must look 'im in the face;
   Nine 'undred of 'is county an' the Regiment's disgrace,
   While they're hangin' Danny Deever in the mornin'.

'What's that so black agin the sun?' said Files-on-Parade.
'It's Danny fightin' 'ard for life,' the Colour-Sergeant said.
'What's that that whimpers over'ead?' said Files-on-Parade.
'It's Danny's soul that's passin' now,' the Colour-Sergeant said.
   For they're done with Danny Deever, you can 'ear the quickstep
     play,
   The Regiment's in column, an' they're marchin' us away;
   Ho! the young recruits are shakin', an' they'll want their beer
     today,
   After hangin' Danny Deever in the mornin'!

THIRTEEN

Early Twentieth Century
1914-39

Turning and turning in the widening gyre
The falcon cannot hear the falconer;
Things fall apart; the centre cannot hold;
Mere anarchy is loosed upon the world,
The blood-dimmed tide is loosed, and everywhere
The ceremony of innocence is drowned;
The best lack all conviction, while the worst
Are full of passionate intensity . . .

Those lines from 'The Second Coming' were written by W. B. Yeats in the long shadow of the end of the First World War, not long before T. S. Eliot wrote *The Waste Land*. Indeed, the Great War of 1914–18 can be seen to mark not only a political divide but a literary one.

And yet of course changes in poetry, or in any of the arts, never work quite as simply as that. Yeats himself was a man who constructed his own poetic world slowly and painfully through a long lifetime of experience. In 1900, when he was thirty-five, he had a reasonably secure minor reputation as a poet who was delicate, melancholy and fond of dreamy and faery-like Irish themes. Gradually he changed, by deliberately coming to terms with his own diversity: he willed himself into greatness, with a toughness of spirit and with the sharpening of his own verbal and rhythmical technique. He learned to speak directly – sometimes through the imagined voice of someone else, as in a poem of the First World War, 'An Irish Airman Foresees His Death':

An Irish Airman Foresees His Death

I know that I shall meet my fate
Somewhere among the clouds above;
Those that I fight I do not hate,
Those that I guard I do not love;

115. W. B. Yeats
painted in 1907
by Augustus John.

My country is Kiltartan Cross,
My countrymen Kiltartan's poor,
No likely end could bring them loss
Or leave them happier than before.
Nor law, nor duty bade me fight,
Nor public men, nor cheering crowds,
A lonely impulse of delight
Drove to this tumult in the clouds;
I balanced all, brought all to mind,
The years to come seemed waste of breath,
A waste of breath the years behind
In balance with this life, this death.

That tragic sense, that sense of heroism which had nothing to do with 'public men' or 'cheering crowds', went alongside Yeats's tragic sense of history itself being a series of patterns of behaviour and action. Man, as Yeats saw him, is controlled by forces of destiny outside himself; the cycles (or 'gyres') of history are continually turning, dragging in their wake a succession of consequences; what has happened will happen again.

This pattern of destiny is the theme of two of his strangest and most powerful poems. In 'The Second Coming' history has reached a point at which the pattern seems to be breaking up, 'Mere anarchy is loosed upon the world', as if some new cosmic revelation is about to be shown – a kind of ghastly parody of Christ coming again into the world:

The Second Coming

Turning and turning in the widening gyre
The falcon cannot hear the falconer;
Things fall apart; the centre cannot hold;
Mere anarchy is loosed upon the world,
The blood-dimmed tide is loosed, and everywhere
The ceremony of innocence is drowned;
The best lack all conviction, while the worst
Are full of passionate intensity.

Surely some revelation is at hand;
Surely the Second Coming is at hand.
The Second Coming! Hardly are those words out
When a vast image out of Spiritus Mundi
Troubles my sight: somewhere in sands of the desert
A shape with lion body and the head of a man,
A gaze blank and pitiless as the sun,
Is moving its slow thighs, while all about it
Reel shadows of the indignant desert birds.
The darkness drops again; but now I know
That twenty centuries of stony sleep
Were vexed to nightmare by a rocking cradle,
And what rough beast, its hour come round at last,
Slouches towards Bethlehem to be born?

'The Second Coming' is a baleful vision of the future. Yeats's poem 'Leda and the Swan' is a concentrated vision of the past, and of one particular moment in the mythical past, organised as in a painting by Michelangelo. According to Greek legend, Leda, a beautiful Queen of

116. 'Leda and the Swan', a copy after the painting by Michelangelo which
was destroyed, on grounds of indecency, in France in the seventeenth century.

Sparta, was noticed by Zeus, the greatest of the gods on Olympus, who
descended to earth in the form of a swan and raped her. From that act,
Helen was born – Helen, whose seduction by Paris was the cause of the
Trojan War, which in its turn caused the birth of the Greek nation, which
in its turn laid the foundations of modern Europe . . . and so on.

Implicit in the picture and in the act itself is the realisation that from it
will result Love and War, the two activities which Helen symbolises; so
that the birth of western civilisation is also the birth of two of man's
primary passions, lust and violence. Zeus, as the supreme god, must have
realised these consequences; but did Leda, the passive woman through
whom history enacted itself?

Leda and the Swan

A sudden blow: the great wings beating still
Above the staggering girl, her thighs caressed
By the dark webs, her nape caught in his bill,
He holds her helpless breast upon his breast.

How can those terrified vague fingers push
The feathered glory from her loosening thighs?
And how can body, laid in that white rush,
But feel the strange heart beating where it lies?

A shudder in the loins engenders there
The broken wall, the burning roof and tower
And Agamemnon dead.
　　　　　　　　Being so caught up,
So mastered by the brute blood of the air,
Did she put on his knowledge with his power
Before the indifferent beak could let her drop?

　　As Yeats grew older, he seemed sometimes to reject any view of man
and woman other than as simple, desiring animals. The 'responsibilities'
of politics, in particular of Irish politics in the struggle against the English
for independence, had much exercised him for many years. But as an
old man he wrote his poem 'Politics', taking some words by the
twentieth-century German novelist, Thomas Mann, as his ironical
epigraph: 'In our time the destiny of man presents its meaning in political
terms'.
　　The scene is a party, full of distinguished, knowledgeable and
opinionated men – politicians, men of affairs, journalists – discussing the
world situation. This was the mid-1930s, the time of the Spanish Civil
War, a rehearsal of confrontation between Fascism, Nazism and Soviet
Communism, with a greater war on the horizon. But something distracts
Yeats from the abstract talk of such things:

Politics

How can I, that girl standing there,
My attention fix
On Roman or on Russian
Or on Spanish politics?
Yet here's a travelled man that knows
What he talks about,
And there's a politician
That has read and thought,
And maybe what they say is true
Of war and war's alarms,
But O that I were young again
And held her in my arms!

When Yeats wrote that, the Second World War was about to break out; but it was a world still haunted by the Great War of 1914–18. Millions had died, in a vast and bloody confusion of national aspirations and conflicting heroisms. But one young man, Wilfred Owen, killed in France at the age of twenty-five in 1918, in the last week of the war, wrote differently in the preface to a book of poems he never saw published:

> This book is not about heroes. English poetry is not yet fit to speak of them. Nor is it about legends, or lands, or anything about glory, honour, might, majesty, dominion, or power, except war. Above all, I am not concerned with poetry. My subject is war, and the pity of war. The poetry is in the pity.

117. Wilfred Owen, one of the important new poetic voices to emerge during the First World War.

118. 'What passing bells for these who die as cattle?'
A corpse on the battlefield of Third Ypres, September 1917.

And here is Owen's 'Anthem for Doomed Youth':

Anthem for Doomed Youth

What passing-bells for these who die as cattle?
  Only the monstrous anger of the guns.
Only the stuttering rifles' rapid rattle
  Can patter out their hasty orisons.
No mockeries now for them; no prayers nor bells,
  Nor any voice of mourning save the choirs, –
The shrill, demented choirs of wailing shells;
  And bugles calling for them from sad shires.

What candles may be held to speed them all?
  Not in the hands of boys, but in their eyes
  Shall shine the holy glimmers of good-byes.
The pallor of girls' brows shall be their pall;
  Their flowers the tenderness of patient minds,
  And each slow dusk a drawing-down of blinds.

That elegiac feeling for the futility of war, tinged with something both bitter and sardonic, is more fully explored by Owen in his dream-like, visionary poem, 'Strange Meeting', about encountering someone who at one level is 'the enemy' but who at another, deeper level is a fellow human being:

Strange Meeting

It seemed that out of battle I escaped
Down some profound dull tunnel, long since scooped
Through granites which titanic wars had groined.
Yet also there encumbered sleepers groaned,
Too fast in thought or death to be bestirred.
Then, as I probed them, one sprang up, and stared
With piteous recognition in fixed eyes,
Lifting distressful hands as if to bless.
And by his smile, I knew that sullen hall,
By his dead smile I knew we stood in Hell.
With a thousand pains that vision's face was grained;
Yet no blood reached there from the upper ground,
And no guns thumped, or down the flues made moan.
'Strange friend,' I said, 'here is no cause to mourn.'
'None,' said that other, 'save the undone years,
The hopelessness. Whatever hope is yours,
Was my life also; I went hunting wild
After the wildest beauty in the world,
Which lies not calm in eyes, or braided hair,
But mocks the steady running of the hour,
And if it grieves, grieves richlier than here.
For of my glee might many men have laughed,
And of my weeping something had been left,
Which must die now. I mean the truth untold,
The pity of war, the pity war distilled.
Now men will go content with what we spoiled,
Or, discontent, boil bloody, and be spilled.
They will be swift with swiftness of the tigress.
None will break ranks, though nations trek from
   progress.
Courage was mine, and I had mystery,
Wisdom was mine, and I had mastery:
To miss the march of this retreating world
Into vain citadels that are not walled.
Then, when much blood had clogged their chariot-
   wheels,

I would go up and wash them from sweet wells,
Even with truths that lie too deep for taint.
I would have poured my spirit without stint
But not through wounds; not on the cess of war.
Foreheads of men have bled where no wounds were.
I am the enemy you killed, my friend.
I knew you in this dark: for so you frowned
Yesterday through me as you jabbed and killed.
I parried; but my hands were loath and cold.
Let us sleep now. . . .'

Another poet killed in the First World War was Edward Thomas. He was already thirty-six when war broke out, and he wrote most of his poetry between then and his death in 1917. Very few of Thomas's poems have anything directly to do with war and battle as Wilfred Owen's do. Thomas searches out scenes and events and feelings in a tentative, hesitant and yet precise way, in which ordinariness and mystery coexist. He thinks of a shrub, one that is sometimes called 'Old Man', growing by the door of his house in England:

Old Man

Old Man, or Lad's-love, – in the name there's nothing
To one that knows not Lad's-love, or Old Man,
The hoar-green feathery herb, almost a tree,
Growing with rosemary and lavender.
Even to one that knows it well, the names
Half decorate, half perplex, the thing it is:
At least, what that is clings not to the names
In spite of time. And yet I like the names.

The herb itself I like not, but for certain
I love it, as some day the child will love it
Who plucks a feather from the door-side bush
Whenever she goes in or out of the house.
Often she waits there, snipping the tips and shrivelling
The shreds at last on to the path, perhaps
Thinking, perhaps of nothing, till she sniffs
Her finger and runs off. The bush is still
But half as tall as she, though it is as old;
So well she clips it. Not a word she says;
And I can only wonder how much hereafter
She will remember, with that bitter scent,

119. Edward Thomas
had published critical
biographies and nature
studies before he
began to write poetry.

Of garden rows, and ancient damson trees
Topping a hedge, a bent path to a door,
A low thick bush beside the door, and me
Forbidding her to pick.
                                    As for myself,
Where first I met the bitter scent is lost.
I, too, often shrivel the grey shreds,
Sniff them and think and sniff again and try
Once more to think what it is I am remembering,
Always in vain. I cannot like the scent,
Yet I would rather give up others more sweet,
With no meaning, than this bitter one.
I have mislaid the key. I sniff the spray
And think of nothing; I see and I hear nothing;
Yet seem, too, to be listening, lying in wait
For what I should, yet never can, remember:
No garden appears, no path, no hoar-green bush
Of Lad's-love, or Old Man, no child beside,
Neither father nor mother, nor any playmate;
Only an avenue, dark, nameless, without end.

Edward Thomas was given the initiative and confidence to write verse by the direct encouragement of an American friend who was living in England in the years immediately before the war and at the beginning of it: Robert Frost. Frost, like Thomas, was a countryman; and in Frost's poems the seasons, the weather, the recurring acts of digging and planting and fencing, all become metaphors for the continuity and habitualness of life. In what seems to be the simplest way, he suggests things that are not simple at all, as in 'Stopping by Woods on a Snowy Evening':

Stopping by Woods on a Snowy Evening

Whose woods these are I think I know.
His house is in the village, though;
He will not see me stopping here
To watch his woods fill up with snow.

My little horse must think it queer
To stop without a farmhouse near
Between the woods and frozen lake
The darkest evening of the year.

He gives his harness bells a shake
To ask if there is some mistake.
The only other sound's the sweep
Of easy wind and downy flake.

The woods are lovely, dark, and deep,
But I have promises to keep,
And miles to go before I sleep,
And miles to go before I sleep.

120. Robert Frost, formerly a New England farmer,
became one of America's most popular poets.

More copiously and elaborately, but still with colloquial and conversational ease, Frost sets out in 'Mending Wall' an extended metaphor about boundaries, limits, distance and neighbourliness, which effortlessly comes to a conclusion which has the force of a proverb:

Mending Wall

Something there is that doesn't love a wall,
That sends the frozen-ground-swell under it,
And spills the upper boulders in the sun;
And makes gaps even two can pass abreast.
The work of hunters is another thing:
I have come after them and made repair
Where they have left not one stone on a stone,
But they would have the rabbit out of hiding,
To please the yelping dogs. The gaps I mean,
No one has seen them made or heard them made,
But at spring mending-time we find them there.
I let my neighbour know beyond the hill;
And on a day we meet to walk the line
And set the wall between us once again.
We keep the wall between us as we go.
To each the boulders that have fallen to each.
And some are loaves and some so nearly balls
We have to use a spell to make them balance:
'Stay where you are until our backs are turned!'
We wear our fingers rough with handling them.
Oh, just another kind of out-door game,
One on a side. It comes to little more:
There where it is we do not need the wall:
He is all pine and I am apple orchard.
My apple tree will never get across
And eat the cones under his pines, I tell him.
He only says, 'Good fences make good neighbours.'
Spring is the mischief in me, and I wonder
If I could put a notion in his head:
'*Why* do they make good neighbours? Isn't it
Where there are cows? But here there are no cows.
Before I built a wall I'd ask to know
What I was walling in or walling out,
And to whom I was like to give offence.
Something there is that doesn't love a wall,
That wants it down.' I could say 'Elves' to him,
But it's not elves exactly, and I'd rather

He said it for himself. I see him there
Bringing a stone grasped firmly by the top
In each hand, like an old-stone savage armed.
He moves in darkness as it seems to me,
Not of woods only and the shade of trees.
He will not go behind his father's saying,
And he likes having thought of it so well
He says again, 'Good fences make good neighbours.'

Nothing could be more different from the deceptive simplicity of Frost's poems than the long poem first published by another American in 1922 – the most formidable and influential poem of the century so far: *The Waste Land*, by T. S. Eliot.

Eliot had settled in England just about the time Edward Thomas and Robert Frost were meeting and talking. In the war years and just after, he had already published poems (such as 'The Love Song of J. Alfred Prufrock') in which a characteristic Eliot method is apparent – the impressionistic juxtaposition of references to other works, sometimes direct, sometimes oblique: a method associated much more with music than with literature, as in the 'quotation' of a theme by one composer in the work of another.

In *The Waste Land* this musical method of themes and variations coming in again and again is a great part of the pattern of the whole thing. The poem has often been seen primarily as a reflection of twentieth-century disillusionment and despair, and it certainly does include these elements; but it has become increasingly clear that its immediate origins lay in Eliot's personal sense at the time of neurosis, disorder, even breakdown. The strangeness and skill of his transpositions everywhere became accepted as a world view, as a diagnosis of a general sickness.

The Waste Land is also in some sense a drama, like a fragmentary play of which the list of characters has been lost. Its five sections are like the five acts into which a Shakespeare play is divided. But the voices are never quite identified: it is as if they are coming from many directions, in many different places, disembodied and yet present, like a dream.

In the poem's second section, 'A Game of Chess', the beginning deliberately parodies the opening lines of Enobarbus's speech from *Antony and Cleopatra* (see page 52), then becomes a lavish description of a rich woman's boudoir, almost in the manner of a late Elizabethan or Jacobean play. There follows a muffled series of self-enclosed statements, by a neurotic woman and her sardonic, disillusioned partner, which then abruptly stop; and we are in a London pub near closing-time,

121. T. S. Eliot painted in 1938 by Wyndham Lewis.

soon after the First World War, in which a Cockney woman gossips about a neighbour's pregnancy, with the landlord's repeated words sounding like a prophecy of doom:

from The Waste Land
'A Game of Chess'

The Chair she sat in, like a burnished throne,
Glowed on the marble, where the glass
Held up by standards wrought with fruited vines
From which a golden Cupidon peeped out
(Another hid his eyes behind his wing)
Doubled the flames of sevenbranched candelabra
Reflecting light upon the table as
The glitter of her jewels rose to meet it,
From satin cases poured in rich profusion;
In vials of ivory and coloured glass
Unstoppered, lurked her strange synthetic perfumes,
Unguent, powdered, or liquid – troubled, confused
And drowned the sense in odours; stirred by the air
That freshened from the window, these ascended
In fattening the prolonged candle-flames,
Flung their smoke into the laquearia,
Stirring the pattern on the coffered ceiling.
Huge sea-wood fed with copper
Burned green and orange, framed by the coloured stone,
In which sad light a carvèd dolphin swam.
Above the antique mantel was displayed
As though a window gave upon the sylvan scene
The change of Philomel, by the barbarous king
So rudely forced; yet there the nightingale
Filled all the desert with inviolable voice
And still she cried, and still the world pursues,
'Jug Jug' to dirty ears.
And other withered stumps of time
Were told upon the walls; staring forms
Leaned out, leaning, hushing the room enclosed.
Footsteps shuffled on the stair.
Under the firelight, under the brush, her hair
Spread out in fiery points
Glowed into words, then would be savagely still.

'My nerves are bad to-night. Yes, bad. Stay with me.
'Speak to me. Why do you never speak. Speak.
   'What are you thinking of? What thinking? What?
'I never know what you are thinking. Think.'

I think we are in rats' alley
Where the dead men lost their bones.

'What is that noise?'
               The wind under the door.
'What is that noise now? What is the wind doing?'
               Nothing again nothing.

                       'Do
'You know nothing? Do you see nothing? Do you
   remember
'Nothing?'

   I remember
Those are pearls that were his eyes.
'Are you alive, or not? Is there nothing in your head?'
                          But
O O O O that Shakespeherian Rag –
It's so elegant
So intelligent
'What shall I do now? What shall I do?'
'I shall rush out as I am, and walk the street
'With my hair down, so. What shall we do tomorrow?
'What shall we ever do?'
               The hot water at ten.
And if it rains, a closed car at four.
And we shall play a game of chess,
Pressing lidless eyes and waiting for a knock upon the
   door.

When Lil's husband got demobbed, I said –
I didn't mince my words, I said to her myself,
HURRY UP PLEASE ITS TIME
Now Albert's coming back, make yourself a bit smart.
He'll want to know what you done with that money he
   gave you
To get yourself some teeth. He did, I was there.
You have them all out, Lil, and get a nice set,
He said, I swear, I can't bear to look at you.

122. T. S. Eliot,
established as the most
influential poet of his
time, painted by Sir
Francis Kelly.

And no more can't I, I said, and think of poor Albert,
He's been in the army four years, he wants a good time,
And if you don't give it him, there's others will, I said.
Oh is there, she said. Something o' that, I said.
Then I'll know who to thank, she said, and give me a
    straight look.
HURRY UP PLEASE ITS TIME
If you don't like it you can get on with it, I said.
Others can pick and choose if you can't.
But if Albert makes off, it won't be for lack of telling.
You ought to be ashamed, I said, to look so antique.
(And her only thirty-one.)
I can't help it, she said, pulling a long face,
It's them pills I took, to bring it off, she said.
(She's had five already, and nearly died of young
    George.)
The chemist said it would be all right, but I've never
    been the same.
You are a proper fool, I said.
Well, if Albert won't leave you alone, there it is, I said,
What you get married for if you don't want children?
HURRY UP PLEASE ITS TIME
Well, that Sunday Albert was home, they had a hot
    gammon,
And they asked me in to dinner, to get the beauty of it
    hot –
HURRY UP PLEASE ITS TIME
HURRY UP PLEASE ITS TIME
Goonight Bill. Goonight Lou. Goonight May. Goonight.
Ta ta. Goonight. Goonight.
Good night, ladies, goodnight, sweet ladies, good night,
    good night.

    It is not too much to say that Eliot's *Waste Land* changed the course of poetry in this century, not only in Britain and America, but in many other parts of the world where it was translated and imitated. No poet can afford quite to ignore it. Certainly the writer who succeeded Eliot as the most influential Anglo-American poet of our time acknowledged its importance to him.

    Yet W. H. Auden was an original of his own kind, a dazzling master of many different voices and manners, who had a very wide appeal, from his early days at the beginning of the 1930s right down to his death in 1973 and beyond. Auden was 'modern', he spoke of the time in which he lived;

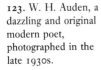

123. W. H. Auden, a dazzling and original modern poet, photographed in the late 1930s.

and yet he did not seem to presuppose the apparatus of scholarship and learning that *The Waste Land* appeared to present.

Sometimes it is as if he is thinking through a problem with his audience – as in his poem 'Musée des Beaux Arts'. It is December 1938: it is already clear that another colossal war is not far off. He is in an art gallery, the Musée des Beaux Arts in Brussels, looking at paintings by the great masters. What he sees seems to put human suffering – and art – into perspective:

Musée des Beaux Arts

About suffering they were never wrong,
The Old Masters: how well they understood
Its human position; how it takes place
While someone else is eating or opening a window or
    just walking dully along;

How, when the aged are reverently, passionately waiting
For the miraculous birth, there always must be
Children who did not specially want it to happen, skating
On a pond at the edge of the wood:
They never forgot
That even the dreadful martyrdom must run its course
Anyhow in a corner, some untidy spot
Where the dogs go on with their doggy
                             life and the torturer's horse
Scratches its innocent behind on a tree.
In Brueghel's Icarus, for instance; how everything turns
    away
Quite leisurely from the disaster; the ploughman may
Have heard the splash, the forsaken cry,
But for him it was not an important failure; the sun
    shone
As it had to on the white legs disappearing into the
    green
Water; and the expensive delicate ship that must have
    seen
Something amazing, a boy falling out of the sky,
Had somewhere to get to and sailed calmly on.

124. Brueghel's 'Landscape with the fall of Icarus'. Icarus has fallen into the sea near the bottom right-hand corner; only his leg and some feathers are visible.

That same year, 1938, Auden wrote a sequence of sonnets called *In Time of War*. He had already seen war at first-hand, in Spain and China; indeed, part of the sequence was written in China. But it is not really *about* war, as such, but about man's predicament in the twentieth century, about the position that human destiny seems to have reached. Each sonnet can stand by itself, yet all interrelate. From the twenty-one that make up the sequence, I have chosen No. VIII. As in all the poems, it is clear that 'He' is man in general, not one particular person:

> He turned his field into a meeting-place,
> And grew the tolerant ironic eye,
> And formed the mobile money-changer's face,
> And found the notion of equality.
>
> And strangers were as brothers to his clocks,
> And with his spires he made a human sky;
> Museums stored his learning like a box,
> And paper watched his money like a spy.
>
> It grew so fast his life was overgrown,
> And he forgot what once it had been made for,
> And gathered into crowds and was alone,
>
> And lived expensively and did without,
> And could not find the earth which he had paid for,
> Nor feel the love that he knew all about.

Two of Auden's contemporaries at Oxford when they were all young together in the late 1920s were Louis MacNeice and John Betjeman. MacNeice, like Auden, was an observant 'social' poet, well aware of what was going on in the world of affairs; but many of his best poems, including his later ones, draw on the past, on common emotions, and on his own childhood and personal experiences. In him, there was a tension between the gregarious, genial man on the one hand and the melancholy solitary on the other. One of his poems written in the 1950s is an almost dream-like (or nightmare-like) re-creation of childhood, 'Soap Suds':

Soap Suds

This brand of soap has the same smell as once in the
    big
House he visited when he was eight: the walls of the
    bathroom open
To reveal a lawn where a great yellow ball rolls back
    through a hoop
To rest at the head of a mallet held in the hands of a
    child.

And these were the joys of that house: a tower with a
    telescope;
Two great faded globes, one of the earth, one of the
    stars;
A stuffed black dog in the hall; a walled garden with
    bees;
A rabbit warren; a rockery; a vine under glass; the sea.

To which he has now returned. The day of course is
    fine
And a grown-up voice cries Play! The mallet slowly
    swings,
Then crack, a great gong booms from the dog-dark hall
    and the ball
Skims forward through the hoop and then through the
    next and then

Through hoops where no hoops were and each dissolves
    in turn
And the grass has grown head-high and an angry voice
    cries Play!
But the ball is lost and the mallet slipped long since
    from the hands
Under the running tap that are not the hands of a child.

    John Betjeman was also a poet who frequently went back to childhood
for the themes of his poems, most extensively in his long reminiscent poem,
Summoned By Bells. Betjeman is often thought of as a comic poet, a writer
of light verse, and he is indeed very funny and often very sharp. But in
'NW5 and N6' (recalling the postal district of London where he lived as a
child) there is a piercing nostalgia, and terror mixed with that nostalgia:

NW5 & N6

Red cliffs arise. And up them service lifts
Soar with the groceries to silver heights.
Lissenden Mansions. And my memory sifts
Lilies from lily-like electric lights
And Irish stew-smells from the smell of prams
And roar of seas from roar of London trams.

Out of it all my memory carves the quiet
Of that dark privet hedge where pleasures breed,
There first, intent upon its leafy diet,
I watched the looping caterpillar feed
And saw it hanging in a gummy froth
Till, weeks on, from the chrysalis burst the moth.

I see black oak twigs outlined on the sky,
Red squirrels on the Burdett-Coutts estate.
I ask my nurse the question 'Will I die?'
As bells from sad St Anne's ring out so late,
'And if I do die, will I go to Heaven?'
Highgate at eventide. Nineteen-eleven.

'You will. I won't.' From that cheap nursery-maid,
Sadist and puritan as now I see,
I first learned what it was to be afraid,
Forcibly fed when sprawled across her knee
Lock'd into cupboards, left alone all day,
'World without end.' What fearsome words to pray.

'World without end.' It was not what she'ld do
That frightened me so much as did her fear
And guilt at endlessness. I caught them too,
Hating to think of sphere succeeding sphere
Into eternity and God's dread will
I caught her terror then. I have it still.

125. Sir John Betjeman,
Poet Laureate 1972–84, photographed in 1961.

FOURTEEN

Later Twentieth Century
1934-84

Do not go gentle into that good night,
Old age should burn and rave at close of day;
Rage, rage against the dying of the light.

Though wise men at their end know dark is right,
Because their words had forked no lightning they
Do not go gentle into that good night . . .

Dylan Thomas's elegy for his dying father, written in 1951, was cast in a form (that of the villanelle, originally from medieval French Provence) which Chaucer would have recognised almost six centuries earlier. As has been apparent throughout this book, every age has its new poetry, but there is always a continuity with the past as well. A poet speaks in his or her own voice, but poets are inevitably both parts of the time they live in and also the inheritors of what has gone before.

This was very true of Dylan Thomas. From his late teens until he died at the age of thirty-nine, his eloquent and sometimes difficult poems drew on a small but intense range of traditional themes: sex, birth, death, nostalgia for lost childhood. Many of Thomas's poems begin with the assumption or insistence that we start to die from the moment we are born – even, indeed, from the moment we are conceived. This continual process of birth and death links us with everything else in the world: the death of a flower comes under the same edict and force as our own death, because the powers of destruction are one. This is the whole burden of one of his best-known early poems, written when he was only eighteen:

The Force that through the Green Fuse Drives the Flower

The force that through the green fuse drives the flower
Drives my green age; that blasts the roots of trees
Is my destroyer.
And I am dumb to tell the crooked rose
My youth is bent by the same wintry fever.

The force that drives the water through the rocks
Drives my red blood; that dries the mouthing streams
Turns mine to wax.
And I am dumb to mouth unto my veins
How at the mountain spring the same mouth sucks.

The hand that whirls the water in the pool
Stirs the quicksand; that ropes the blowing wind
Hauls my shroud sail.
And I am dumb to tell the hanging man
How of my clay is made the hangman's lime.

The lips of time leech to the fountain head;
Love drips and gathers, but the fallen blood
Shall calm her sores.
And I am dumb to tell a weather's wind
How time has ticked a heaven round the stars.

And I am dumb to tell the lover's tomb
How at my sheet goes the same crooked worm.

Dylan Thomas was a legend in his own lifetime, and became an even more powerful legend after his death in 1953 – yet another Romantic image of the poet as disreputable drunkard, licensed jester and self-destroyer. When he died, there were such headlines in the newspapers as 'The Poet They Called a Dangerous Cherub' and 'The Most Fantastic Character of Our Time'. But the legend mainly had to do with Thomas's behaviour, not with his poems, which are almost without exception skilled and serious pieces of craftsmanship. He was a prodigy who began to burn out early; he had created much of his best work by the time he was twenty-one. But towards the end of his life, his elegy for his father stands out:

126. Dylan Thomas painted by Augustus John,
looking very much like 'a dangerous cherub'.

Do Not Go Gentle into That Good Night

Do not go gentle into that good night,
Old age should burn and rave at close of day;
Rage, rage against the dying of the light.

Though wise men at their end know dark is right,
Because their words had forked no lightning they
Do not go gentle into that good night.

Good men, the last wave by, crying how bright
Their frail deeds might have danced in a green bay,
Rage, rage against the dying of the light.

Wild men who caught and sang the sun in flight,
And learn, too late, they grieved it on its way,
Do not go gentle into that good night.

Grave men, near death, who see with blinding sight
Blind eyes could blaze like meteors and be gay,
Rage, rage against the dying of the light.

And you, my father, there on the sad height,
Curse, bless, me now with your fierce tears, I pray.
Do not go gentle into that good night.
Rage, rage against the dying of the light.

Across the Atlantic, a very slightly younger contemporary of Dylan
Thomas began to be recognised as one of America's finest poets at about
the time of Thomas's death. Robert Lowell came from a family in New
England which ancestrally had been involved with what was called 'the
New England Renaissance' of the nineteenth century. But Lowell broke
away on his own, as a young man going elsewhere to learn from poets he
admired, such as Allen Tate and John Crowe Ransom.

From his early years, too, he was afflicted with recurring bouts of
mental disorder, manic attacks over which he had little control, which left
him (as he put it) 'tamed and tranquillised', but which increasingly
became both part of his creative energy and to some extent his
subject-matter, right up to his death in 1977.

Lowell's breakthrough, into poems which drew on his New England
family and his own life, and which quietly and intimately come to terms
with his own disturbance, can be seen in the publication of his book *Life
Studies* in 1959. In it, he faced the experience directly, in a way that has
been called 'confessional': as in his poem 'Skunk Hour', in which a small
New England town becomes almost a vision of hell:

Skunk Hour

Nautilus Island's hermit
heiress still lives through winter in her Spartan cottage;
her sheep still graze above the sea.
Her son's a bishop. Her farmer
is first selectman in our village,
she's in her dotage.

Thirsting for
the hierarchic privacy
of Queen Victoria's century,
she buys up all
the eyesores facing her shore,
and lets them fall.

The season's ill –
we've lost our summer millionaire,
who seemed to leap from an L. L. Bean
catalogue. His nine-knot yawl
was auctioned off to lobstermen.
A red fox stain covers Blue Hill.

And now our fairy
decorator brightens his shop for fall,
his fishnet's filled with orange cork,
orange, his cobbler's bench and awl,
there is no money in his work,
he'd rather marry.

One dark night,
my Tudor Ford climbed the hill's skull,
I watched for love-cars. Lights turned down,
they lay together, hull to hull,
where the graveyard shelves on the town. . . .
My mind's not right.

A car radio bleats,
'Love, O careless Love . . .' I hear
my ill-spirit sob in each blood cell,
as if my hand were at its throat . . .
I myself am hell
nobody's here –

only skunks, that search
in the moonlight for a bite to eat.
They march on their soles up Main Street:
white stripes, moonstruck eyes' red fire
under the chalk-dry and spar spire
of the Trinitarian Church.

I stand on top
of our back steps and breathe the rich air –
a mother skunk with her column of kittens swills the
    garbage pail.
She jabs her wedge head in a cup
of sour cream, drops her ostrich tail,
and will not scare.

127. Robert Lowell, one of America's finest modern poets, achieved recognition in the 1950s.

But Lowell was not just a personal and self-obsessed poet, marvellously skilful though he was with his own obsessions. He could see his own disturbances as the reflections of something bigger, in the disturbances of history and the present day, in the sufferings which are part of the fabric of politics and society. There is nothing abstract in Lowell's poems on these larger public themes: they are crowded with images of the real, the observed – real people and real places, from the past and the present.

In his poem 'For the Union Dead', he takes his title from a war memorial, one of the countless memorials put up after the American Civil War: in this case the monument in Boston which commemorates the black infantrymen who fought on the Northern, or Union, side under the command of their white officer, Colonel Shaw. Lowell can see before his eyes the Boston of his childhood changing, the earth-moving machines literally creating a new world – a world of money and opportunism, in which the old frayed ideals are cynically disregarded:

For the Union Dead

The old South Boston Aquarium stands
in a Sahara of snow now. Its broken windows are
    boarded.
The bronze weathervane cod has lost its scales.
The airy tanks are dry.

Once my nose crawled like a snail on the glass;
my hand tingled
to burst the bubbles
drifting from the noses of the cowed, compliant fish.

My hand draws back. I often sigh still
for the dark downward and vegetating kingdom
of the fish and reptile. One morning last March,
I pressed against the new barbed and galvanized

fence on the Boston Common. Behind their cage,
yellow dinosaur steamshovels were grunting
as they cropped up tons of mush and grass
to gouge their underworld garage.

Parking spaces luxuriate like civic
sandpiles in the heart of Boston.
A girdle of orange, Puritan-pumpkin colored girders
braces the tingling Statehouse,

shaking over the excavations, as it faces Colonel Shaw
and his bell-cheeked Negro infantry
on St Gaudens' shaking Civil War relief,
propped by a plank splint against the garage's
    earthquake.

Two months after marching through Boston,
half the regiment was dead;
at the dedication,
William James could almost hear the bronze Negroes
    breathe.

Their monument sticks like a fishbone
in the city's throat.
Its Colonel is as lean
as a compass-needle.

He has an angry wrenlike vigilance,
a greyhound's gentle tautness;
he seems to wince at pleasure,
and suffocate for privacy.

He is out of bounds now. He rejoices in man's lovely,
peculiar power to choose life and die –
when he leads his black soldiers to death,
he cannot bend his back.

On a thousand small town New England greens,
the old white churches hold their air
of sparse, sincere rebellion; frayed flags
quilt the graveyards of the Grand Army of the Republic.

The stone statues of the abstract Union Soldier
grow slimmer and younger each year –
wasp-waisted, they doze over muskets
and muse through their sideburns . . .

Shaw's father wanted no monument
except the ditch,
where his son's body was thrown
and lost with his 'niggers.'

The ditch is nearer.
There are no statues for the last war here;
on Boyleston Street, a commercial photograph
shows Hiroshima boiling

over a Mosler Safe, the 'Rock of Ages'
that survived the blast. Space is nearer.
When I crouch to my television set,
the drained faces of Negro school-children rise like
     balloons.

Colonel Shaw
is riding on his bubble,
he waits
for the blesséd break.

The Aquarium is gone. Everywhere,
giant finned cars nose forward like fish;
a savage servility
slides by on grease.

Lowell's troubled, unresolved nostalgia for something that is going, and maybe has already gone forever, can be seen in different form in another famous poem of our own time by one of the best living English poets: 'Church Going', by Philip Larkin.

Just as Lowell's 'For the Union Dead' is partly a meditation on the death of political idealism, so Larkin's poem is a meditation on the death of religious faith. Like Lowell's poem, Larkin's is full of sharp and specific details, so that it grows out of a whole cluster of particularities: a real place at a real time – here, an empty church into which an unbelieving visitor steps, casually and a bit warily. He moves from mocking indifference to puzzled indifference, and in the end towards a position which, though it hardly endorses the mysteries for which the place was built, accepts seriously the human 'hunger' for ritual and order which is enshrined there:

Church Going

Once I am sure there's nothing going on
I step inside, letting the door thud shut.
Another church: matting, seats, and stone,
And little books; sprawlings of flowers, cut
For Sunday, brownish now; some brass and stuff

128. Philip Larkin
photographed in 1958.

Up at the holy end; the small neat organ;
And a tense, musty, unignorable silence,
Brewed God knows how long. Hatless, I take off
My cycle-clips in awkward reverence,

Move forward, run my hand around the font.
From where I stand, the roof looks almost new –
Cleaned, or restored? Someone would know: I don't.
Mounting the lectern, I peruse a few
Hectoring large-scale verses, and pronounce
'Here endeth' much more loudly than I'd meant.
The echoes snigger briefly. Back at the door
I sign the book, donate an Irish sixpence,
Reflect the place was not worth stopping for.

Yet stop I did: in fact I often do,
And always end much at a loss like this,
Wondering what to look for; wondering, too,
When churches fall completely out of use
What we shall turn them into, if we shall keep
A few cathedrals chronically on show,
Their parchment, plate and pyx in locked cases,
And let the rest rent-free to rain and sheep.
Shall we avoid them as unlucky places?

Or, after dark, will dubious women come
To make their children touch a particular stone;
Pick simples for a cancer; or on some
Advised night see walking a dead one?
Power of some sort or other will go on
In games, in riddles, seemingly at random;
But superstition, like belief, must die,
And what remains when disbelief has gone?
Grass, weedy pavement, brambles, buttress, sky,

A shape less recognisable each week,
A purpose more obscure. I wonder who
Will be the last, the very last, to seek
This place for what it was; one of the crew
That tap and jot and know what rood-lofts were?
Some ruin-bibber, randy for antique,
Or Christmas-addict, counting on a whiff
Of gown-and-bands and organ-pipes and myrrh?
Or will he be my representative,

129. Larkin, recognised as the most distinguished voice of a new generation of twentieth century poets, photographed in 1983.

Bored, uninformed, knowing the ghostly silt
Dispersed, yet tending to this cross of ground
Through suburb scrub because it held unspilt
So long and equably what since is found
Only in separation – marriage, and birth,
And death, and thoughts of these – for which was built
This special shell? For, though I've no idea
What this accoutred frowsty barn is worth,
It pleases me to stand in silence here;

A serious house on serious earth it is,
In whose blent air all our compulsions meet,
Are recognised, and robed as destinies.
And that much never can be obsolete,
Since someone will forever be surprising
A hunger in himself to be more serious,
And gravitating with it to this ground,
Which, he once heard, was proper to grow wise in,
If only that so many dead lie round.

As has been plain in much of the poetry in this book, poets can summon up an incident (a 'story', if you like) in a way that is more condensed, more economical and more vivid than a novelist or story-writer can. Philip Larkin in 'Church Going' uses something of a story-teller's technique in his strategy of placing the reader in the position of walking into the church and round it, looking at things, wondering what they mean, and coming to a serious conclusion but one that is still open, still unresolved.

In another poem, Larkin imagines a particular moment at a particular time in the recent past, perhaps in the 1920s, which in only twenty-five lines he fixes forever: a moment of vision of life, and death, and life-in-death:

The Explosion

On the day of the explosion
Shadows pointed towards the pithead:
In the sun the slagheap slept.

Down the lane came men in pitboots
Coughing oath-edged talk and pipe-smoke,
Shouldering off the freshened silence.

One chased after rabbits; lost them;
Came back with a nest of lark's eggs;
Showed them; lodged them in the grasses.

So they passed in beards and moleskins,
Fathers, brothers, nicknames, laughter,
Through the tall gates standing open.

At noon, there came a tremor; cows
Stopped chewing for a second; sun,
Scarfed as in a heat-haze, dimmed.

The dead go on before us, they
Are sitting in God's house in comfort,
We shall see them face to face –

Plain as lettering in the chapels
It was said, and for a second
Wives saw men of the explosion

Larger than in life they managed –
Gold as on a coin, or walking
Somehow from the sun towards them,

One showing the eggs unbroken.

Robert Graves is a poet of an earlier generation than Larkin's; he was already writing well when he was a young officer in France during the First World War (when he was officially reported dead of wounds on his twenty-first birthday). But his is a reputation that has grown with time, and his subtle individuality and timelessness have gradually established themselves. In 'The Cool Web', he examines lyrically and gently both the limitations and the strength of language – how it inhibits us and expresses us:

The Cool Web

Children are dumb to say how hot the day is,
How hot the scent is of the summer rose,
How dreadful the black wastes of evening sky,
How dreadful the tall soldiers drumming by.

130. Robert Graves, who is highly regarded both as the author of such books as *Goodbye to All That* and *I, Claudius*, and as a poet.

But we have speech, to chill the angry day,
And speech, to dull the rose's cruel scent.
We spell away the overhanging night,
We spell away the soldiers and the fright.

There's a cool web of language winds us in,
Retreat from too much joy or too much fear:
We grow sea-green at last and coldly die
In brininess and volubility.

But if we let our tongues lose self-possession,
Throwing off language and its watery clasp
Before our death, instead of when death comes,
Facing the wide glare of the children's day,
Facing the rose, the dark sky and the drums,
We shall go mad no doubt and die that way.

A word that has hardly been used in this book is the word 'inspiration'. Yet it is a word that many people would automatically associate with poetry and poets, as a way of describing the mysterious force that is supposed to come to a poet, the undefinable thing that starts him off. It is perhaps because it *is* mysterious and undefinable that I have avoided using it. But the way in which a poem comes to a poet, the way in which (to use an old-fashioned phrase) he is 'visited by the Muse', is the very subject of a poem by another living English poet, Ted Hughes. In 'The Thought-Fox', Hughes captures in the image of a fox the power of creation, the moment of resolution that arrives with the making of a poem:

The Thought-Fox

I imagine this midnight moment's forest:
Something else is alive
Beside the clock's loneliness
And this blank page where my fingers move.

Through the window I see no star:
Something more near
Though deeper within darkness
Is entering the loneliness:

Cold, delicately as the dark snow
A fox's nose touches twig, leaf;
Two eyes serve a movement, that now
And again now, and now, and now

Sets neat prints into the snow
Between trees, and warily a lame
Shadow lags by stump and in hollow
Of a body that is bold to come

Across clearings, an eye,
A widening deepening greenness,
Brilliantly, concentratedly,
Coming about its own business

Till, with a sudden sharp hot stink of fox
It enters the dark hole of the head.
The window is starless still; the clock ticks,
The page is printed.

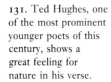

131. Ted Hughes, one of the most prominent younger poets of this century, shows a great feeling for nature in his verse.

The physical immediacy of Ted Hughes's poem is shared by many of Sylvia Plath's. There is no doubt that Hughes and Plath, who were together for six prolific and intense years, had a profound influence on one another's writing. It is natural, though neither accurate nor admirable, that most attention has been focussed on the obsessive, isolated poems of Plath's final months, which produced 'Lady Lazarus' and 'Daddy' – brilliant but narrowly neurotic performances. But she was also an acutely tender writer, as in a poem which looks at an old man convalescing in the spring, 'Among the Narcissi':

Among the Narcissi

Spry, wry, and grey as these March sticks,
Percy bows, in his blue peajacket, among the narcissi.
He is recuperating from something on the lung.

The narcissi, too, are bowing to some big thing:
It rattles their stars on the green hill where Percy
Nurses the hardship of his stitches, and walks and walks.

There is a dignity to this; there is a formality –
The flowers vivid as bandages, and the man mending.
They bow and stand: they suffer such attacks!

And the octogenarian loves the little flocks.
He is quite blue; the terrible wind tries his breathing.
The narcissi look up like children, quickly and whitely.

132. Some of the major poets
of the twentieth century together in 1960
at a party for the publication
of *Homage to Clio* by W. H. Auden.
Left to right: Louis MacNeice, Ted Hughes,
T. S. Eliot and W. H. Auden.

Biographical and Bibliographical Notes

1 Chaucer, 1340 - 1400

Geoffrey
Chaucer
c. 1340–1400

Born in London. While still in his teens, served with the King's forces in France, was captured and ransomed. On his return to England in 1360 was taken into the royal service. Married a lady-in-waiting, 1366. Valet to Edward III, 1367, and Esquire, 1368. Went on diplomatic missions to Italy, 1372 and 1378, and to France, 1377. Controller of Customs and Subsidies on Wools, Skins and Tanned Hides in London, 1374–86. Justice of the Peace, 1385. Knight of the Shire (Member of Parliament) for Kent, 1385–6. In the absence of his chief patron, John of Gaunt, lost these offices, 1387. On Gaunt's return from Spain became Clerk of the King's Works, 1389–91, supervising architects and builders. In 1394 and 1398 granted royal pensions.

Chief works:

1360–72: *The Romaunt of the Rose* (translation from French of the *Roman de la Rose*), *The Book of the Duchesse.*

1373–85: *The House of Fame, The Parlement of Foules, Troilus and Criseyde,* possibly some early versions of some of *The Canterbury Tales.*

1386–1400: *The Legend of Good Women, The Canterbury Tales.*

Modern editions:

The Complete Works of Geoffrey Chaucer, edited by F. N. Robinson (revised edition, 1957).
The Canterbury Tales; a New Translation, by Nevill Coghill (revised edition, 1960).

2 Medieval to Elizabethan, 1400-1600

John Skelton
c. 1460–1529

Probably born in Yorkshire. Educated at Cambridge and probably also Oxford. Official court poet, 1488. Tutor to Prince Henry (later Henry VIII) 1494–1502. Appointed Rector of Diss, 1502, retired there about 1504. Appointed King's Orator and returned to court, 1512.

John Skelton: The Complete English Poems, edited by John Scattergood, 1983.

Sir Thomas
Wyatt
c. 1503–42

Born in Kent. Educated at Cambridge. At court of Henry VIII, Clerk of the King's Jewels, 1524–31. On diplomatic missions to France, 1526, and Papal Court, 1527. Marshal of Calais Castle, 1528–32. Privy Councillor, 1533. Imprisoned on charges of adultery with Anne Boleyn, 1536, and pardoned. Knighted, 1537. Ambassador to Spain and to Emperor Charles V, 1537–9. Missions to France and Holland, 1539–40. Charged with treason and 'papist tendencies' as ally of Thomas Cromwell, 1541: imprisoned, tried and acquitted. Appointed High Steward of the King's manor at Maidstone, Kent, 1542.

Sir Thomas Wyatt: The Complete Poems, edited by R. A. Rebholz, 1978.

Sir Philip
Sidney
1554–86

Born in Kent. Educated at Shrewsbury and Oxford. Travelled in France, Germany and Italy. A member of Queen Elizabeth's court, he became a Member of Parliament in 1581 and was knighted in 1582. He went with the Earl of Leicester's expedition to fight the Spanish in the Netherlands, and died in battle at Zutphen.

Poems, edited by William A. Ringler, 1962.

Edmund
Spenser
c. 1552–99

Born in London. Educated at Cambridge. Joined the household of the Earl of Leicester in his late twenties, and then was appointed Secretary to Lord Grey, Lord Deputy of Ireland. For the rest of his life he held administrative posts in Ireland, until he returned to London the year before his death.

The Poetical Works of Edmund Spenser, edited by J. C. Smith and E. de Selincourt, 1912.

Chidiock Tichborne c. 1558–86	Little is known about his early life. Both he and his father were ardent Catholics. In 1586 he was implicated in the so-called 'Babington Conspiracy' against Queen Elizabeth, was arrested and hanged. The poem included here, his only known piece, is from *Verses of Praise and Joy*, first published in the year of his death.
Thomas Nashe 1567–1601	Born in Suffolk. Educated at Cambridge. In London, wrote many controversial pamphlets on religious, political, social and literary matters. Wrote picaresque novel, *The Unfortunate Traveller*, 1594.
	The Complete Works of Thomas Nashe, edited by F. B. Wilson, 1958.
Christopher Marlowe 1564–93	Born in Kent. Educated at Cambridge. Settled in London, 1587. *Tamburlaine the Great* produced 1587, *Doctor Faustus* 1588 or 1592, four other plays between 1589 and 1593. Charged with sedition and blasphemy before Privy Council, 1593. Stabbed in a Deptford tavern, 1593.
	Christopher Marlowe: The Complete Poems and Translations, edited by Stephen Orgel, 1971.
Sir Walter Raleigh c. 1552–1618	Born in Devon. Educated at Oxford. Fought in France and Ireland, 1569 and 1580. Entered court of Queen Elizabeth, 1581. Knighted 1584. Expeditions to Virginia, 1584–7. Imprisoned in Tower for seducing a maid-of-honour, 1592. Explorations in Caribbean, 1595. Expeditions against Spain, 1596–7. Governor of Jersey, 1600–03. Arrested on treason charge on accession of James I, 1603, and imprisoned in Tower 1603–16. Failed expedition to Guiana, 1617. On his return, executed on former treason charge.
	The Poems of Sir Walter Raleigh, edited by Agnes Latham, 1951.
Michael Drayton 1563–1631	Born in Warwickshire. Chiefly supported throughout his life by noble or royal patronage, by the Admiral's Players 1597–1602, and by other theatre groups. Friend of Marlowe, Ben Jonson and Shakespeare.
	Poems of Michael Drayton, edited by John Buxton, 1953.

3 Shakespeare, 1564-1616

William
Shakespeare
1564–1616

Born in Warwickshire. Probably educated at the
grammar school, Stratford. Settled in London about
1588, and by 1592 well enough known as a playwright to
be insulted by the poet Robert Greene as 'an upstart
crow beautified with our feathers'. Also known as an
actor, mentioned as a leading member of the Lord
Chamberlain's Men in 1595, and closely associated with
this company (later called the King's Men, after the
accession of James I in 1603) for the rest of his
theatrical career. Bought New Place in Stratford in
1597, and continued to buy property there after his
father's death in 1601. Finally settled in Stratford in
1611, the year of the first production of *The Tempest*, his
last play (though he probably had a hand in *Henry VIII*
and *The Two Noble Kinsmen*, both produced in 1613).
Comedies, Histories, and Tragedies (the so-called First
Folio of Shakespeare), edited by John Heming and
Henry Condell, first published after his death in 1623.
Many individual plays appeared in print in his lifetime,
but often in inaccurate and mutilated form. The
following list gives the first publication of his poems, and
the probable date of the first production of each play.

Poems:

Venus and Adonis   1593
The Rape of Lucrece   1594
Sonnets   1609
Poems   1640

Plays:

Henry VI Part 1 ⎫
Henry VI Part 2 ⎬   1590–92
Henry VI Part 3 ⎭
Comedy of Errors   1590
Richard III   1593
The Taming of the Shrew   1593
Titus Andronicus   1594
Two Gentlemen of Verona   1594
King John   1594
A Midsummer Night's Dream   1595
Richard II   1595
Love's Labour's Lost   1596
Romeo and Juliet   1596

The Merchant of Venice   1597
Henry IV Part 1   1597
Henry IV Part 2   1598
As You Like It   1598
Henry V   1599
Julius Caesar   1599
Much Ado About Nothing   1599
Twelfth Night   1600
The Merry Wives of Windsor   1600
Hamlet   1601
Troilus and Cressida   1602
All's Well That Ends Well   1603
Measure for Measure   1604
Othello   1604
King Lear   1605
Macbeth   1605
Timon of Athens   1606
Pericles   1607
Antony and Cleopatra   1607
Coriolanus   1608
Cymbeline   1609
The Winter's Tale   1610
The Tempest   1611

Modern edition: Among many editions of the plays and poems, both individually and in single-volume form, I have found the following most useful:

William Shakespeare: The Complete Works ('The Complete Pelican Shakespeare'), edited by Alfred Harbage, 1969.

4 Metaphysical and Devotional, 1590-1670

John Donne
1572–1631

Born in London. Brought up a Roman Catholic, went very young to Oxford, and finished his education as a law student at Lincoln's Inn. Went on expeditions under the Earl of Essex to Cadiz (1596) and the Azores (1597). Appointed secretary to the Lord Keeper, Sir Thomas Egerton, 1598. Dismissed and disgraced for secret marriage to Egerton's niece, 1601. Sporadically looking for an appointment and patronage, until ordained in the Anglican Church in 1615, largely at the instigation of James I. From then on, a royal chaplain and frequent preacher at court. Appointed Dean of St Paul's, 1622.

John Donne: The Complete English Poems, edited by A. J. Smith, 1971.

George Herbert 1593–1633
Born at Montgomery Castle, Wales. Educated at Cambridge, where he was a Fellow of Trinity College, Reader in Rhetoric, and Public Orator from 1619–27. Frequently at court, 1620–25. Ordained deacon, 1626, and priest, 1630. Rector of Bemerton, Wiltshire, 1630–33.

George Herbert: Works, edited by F. E. Hutchinson, 1945.

Sir John Suckling c. 1609–41
Born in Middlesex. Educated at Cambridge. Inherited his father's estates, 1627. After continental travel, became a court poet and attendant to Charles I. Fought for the King. Having been discovered in a plot in 1641, he fled to Paris, and died there.

Works, edited by Thomas Clayton and L. A. Beaurline, 1971.

Richard Lovelace 1618–58
Born in London. Educated at Charterhouse and Oxford. Became a professional soldier and fought in the Scottish campaigns, 1639–40. Later fought for Charles I during the Civil War, and after the defeat of the Royalists served with the French army against Spain. On his return to England he was imprisoned by Cromwell. Probably died in poverty in London.

Poems, edited by C. H. Wilkinson, 1930.

Robert Herrick c. 1591–1674
Born in London. Apprenticed to his uncle, goldsmith and jeweller, and later attended Cambridge. Ordained in the Church of England, 1623, was vicar of Dean Prior, Devon, 1629–47 (when he was ejected by the Puritans), lived in London 1647–62, and then returned to Dean Prior, where he spent the rest of his life.

Poetical Works of Robert Herrick, edited by L. C. Martin, 1956.

Andrew Marvell 1621–78

Born in Yorkshire. Educated at Cambridge. Travelled in Holland, France, Italy and Spain, partly working as a tutor, 1642–6. Tutor to daughter of Lord Fairfax, Lord-General of Cromwell's Parliamentary Forces, 1650–52, at Nun Appleton House, Yorkshire, where he wrote many of his lyrical poems. Assistant to Milton in the Secretaryship for Foreign Tongues, 1657–8. MP for Hull, 1659–78.

Complete English Poems of Andrew Marvell, edited by Elizabeth Story Donno, 1972.

5 Milton, 1608-74

John Milton 1608–74

Born in London. Educated at Cambridge, after which he studied privately at home, 1632–8. Travelled in France and Italy, 1638–9. Settled in London, taking in private pupils, 1640. Married Mary Powell, 1642; they soon parted, then reunited in 1645, but she died in 1652. From 1641, for twenty years Milton largely wrote prose: tracts and pamphlets on religion, divorce, education, censorship and politics. In 1649, after Charles I's execution, appointed Secretary for Foreign Tongues to Cromwell's Council of State. Began to go blind in about 1650, and his blindness became complete by 1652, but continued to serve in office. Married Katherine Woodcock, 1656; she died in childbirth, 1657. Deprived of all official work at the Restoration of Charles II, 1660. Married Elizabeth Minshull, 1662.

Chief works:

1629 'On the Morning of Christ's Nativity'
1631 'L'Allegro' and 'Il Penseroso'
1634 *Comus*
1638 'Lycidas'
1657(?)–67 *Paradise Lost*
1671 *Paradise Regained* and *Samson Agonistes*

Modern edition: *John Milton: Poems*, edited by John Carey and Alastair Fowler, 1971.

6 Restoration and Augustan, 1660 - 1745

John Wilmot
Earl of Rochester
1647–80

Born in Oxfordshire. Succeeded his father as Earl in 1658. Educated at Oxford. Travelled in France and Italy, 1663–4, under the patronage of Charles II, then came to court, where he quickly established himself as wit, rake, amorist and adventurer. Frequently dismissed, frequently reinstated. Appointed Keeper of Woodstock Park, Oxfordshire, 1674. Retired from court with failing health, 1679. Converted to Christianity and recanted his past life on his deathbed.

Rochester: Complete Poems, edited by D. M. Vieth, 1968.

John Dryden
1631–1700

Born in Northamptonshire. Educated at Cambridge until 1657 when he went to London, where he briefly held a government appointment under Cromwell. From then on, after the Restoration of 1660, he chiefly earned his living as a playwright, beginning with *The Wild Gallant* in 1663 and going on to write over twenty-five plays. Appointed Poet Laureate, 1668.

John Dryden: Poems, edited by James Kinsley, 1958.

Jonathan
Swift
1667–1745

Born in Dublin. Educated at Trinity College, Dublin. Ordained Anglican priest, 1695, and thereafter held various livings in Ireland until appointed Dean of St Patrick's Cathedral, Dublin, 1713. Began writing poems in 1692, pamphlets and journalism in 1701. *A Tale of a Tub*, his first fiction, was published in 1704, and what became known as *Gulliver's Travels* in 1726. Apart from visits to London (1710–14, and more briefly afterwards), he lived in Dublin from 1701 until his death.

The Poems of Jonathan Swift, edited by Harold Williams, 1937.

Alexander
Pope
1688–1744

Born in London. Deformed and stunted from birth, he was largely educated at home: his Roman Catholic upbringing also prevented him from attending university. *An Essay on Criticism*, 1711, made him famous and successful at an early age. Thereafter he worked solely as a writer, translator (the whole of the *Iliad* and the *Odyssey*, 1715–26) and editor (of *The Works of Shakespeare*, 1725).

Alexander Pope: Poetical Works, edited by Herbert Davis, 1966.

7 Late Classical Poets and Romantic Pioneers, 1750-1805

Samuel Johnson 1709–84

Born in Staffordshire. Educated at Lichfield Grammar School and briefly at Oxford. Taught private pupils. Settled in London in 1737 and worked at a variety of things: writing for magazines, editing, compiling his great Dictionary (1747–55), until he was given a royal pension in 1762. Continued to write pamphlets and much else, and travelled a good deal, particularly with James Boswell, who wrote his biography.

Complete English Poems, edited by J. D. Fleeman, 1971.

Thomas Gray 1716–71

Born in London. Educated at Eton and Cambridge, where he became a don in 1741, finally becoming Professor of Modern History in the university in 1768.

Complete English Poems, edited by James Reeves, 1973.

Christopher Smart 1722–71

Born in Kent but spent most of his childhood in Durham. Educated at Cambridge, and became a Fellow of Pembroke Hall in 1745. After a few years of some academic and literary success there, along with some unstable periods, he went to London to write, edit and work for a bookseller. Between 1751 and 1763 he veered between prolonged hack-work and bouts of insanity, being committed to Bedlam in 1763, and finally dying in a debtor's prison in 1771.

Collected Poems, edited by Norman Callan, 1949.
Rejoice in the Lamb (Jubilate Agno): A Song from Bedlam, edited by W. H. Bond, 1954.

William Blake 1757–1827

Born in London. Studied at a drawing-school there, then was apprenticed to an engraver. From 1778, worked as illustrator and graphic designer, and gave drawing lessons. Lived in Felpham, Sussex, with the help of William Hayley, 1800–04. Moved back to London, and lived in obscurity there, doing hack-work, until in the early 1820s several young artists (including Samuel Palmer) adopted and helped him.

William Blake: The Complete Poems, edited by Alicia Ostriker, 1977.

Samuel Taylor Coleridge 1772–1834

Born in Devon. Educated at Cambridge. Joined the army for a short time, but returned to Cambridge. Became friendly with the poet Robert Southey, and married his sister-in-law. Lived in Bristol, 1794–7, and then Somerset, where he first met Wordsworth in 1797. Given an annuity by the Wedgwood family, 1798. Lived with Southey, then with the Wordsworths, in the Lake District, 1800–04. Became addicted to opium about this time. Moved to Highgate, London, 1816, and lived there till his death.

Coleridge: Complete Verse, Select Prose and Letters, edited by Stephen Potter, 1950.

8 Wordsworth, 1770 - 1850

William Wordsworth 1770–1850

Born in Cumberland. Educated there and at Cambridge. Lived in France, 1791–2. Lived with his sister Dorothy in Dorset and Somerset, 1795–7, and toured Germany with Dorothy and Coleridge, 1798–9. Settled with Dorothy at Dove Cottage in Lake District, 1799. Received a legacy in his father's will after long litigation, 1802, and married Mary Hutchinson. Granted the sinecure of Distributor of Stamps for Westmorland, 1813. Publication of his *Poems* in two volumes in 1815 secured his reputation. Appointed Poet Laureate, 1843.

Chief works:

1798	*Lyrical Ballads*, with Coleridge
1800	*Lyrical Ballads*, revised edition, with Wordsworth's preface.
1807	*Poems* (two volumes)
1814	*The Excursion*
1815	*Poems* (two volumes)
1838	*The Sonnets*
1850	*The Prelude*

Modern editions:	*William Wordsworth: The Poems* (two volumes), edited by John O. Hayden, 1977. *The Prelude: A Parallel Text* (1805 and 1850 versions), edited by J. C. Maxwell, 1971.

9 Younger Romantics, 1800 - 24

Percy Bysshe Shelley
1792–1822

Born in Sussex. Educated at Oxford, but expelled for publishing pamphlets on atheism. Eloped with Harriet Westbrook (aged sixteen), had two children, but left Harriet for Mary Wollstonecraft Godwin, whom he married in 1816 after Harriet's suicide. Went to live in Italy, 1818, staying in Rome, Pisa, Leghorn and elsewhere. Drowned in the Bay of Spezia. Published over twenty books of poems, plays, romances, pamphlets etc. in less than a dozen years.

The Poems of Percy Bysshe Shelley, edited by G. M. Matthews, 1970.

John Keats
1795–1821

Born in London. In 1810, after the deaths of first his father and then his mother, apprenticed by his guardian to a surgeon and apothecary. Studied at Guy's Hospital and qualified as apothecary, 1816. At about the same time, met Leigh Hunt, who introduced him to Shelley and others, and at whose encouragement he abandoned medicine in order to write poetry. Published *Poems*, 1817, *Endymion*, 1818, and *Lamia, Isabella, The Eve of St Agnes, and Other Poems*, 1820. Fell ill towards end of 1819, went to Italy to try to recover in 1820, and died in Rome within five months of his departure.

The Poems of John Keats, edited by Miriam Allott, 1970.

George Gordon Lord Byron
1788–1824

Born in London, son of the 6th Baron Byron, whom he succeeded at the age of ten. Educated at Cambridge. Published his first volumes in his late teens. Toured in the Mediterranean, 1809–11; the publication of the first two cantos of *Childe Harold's Pilgrimage* in 1812, prompted by this tour, began his popular success. Married in 1815, but almost immediately began a series of affairs with other women, including possibly his

half-sister Augusta. Because of these scandals, left
England in 1816, going first to Geneva with the
Shelleys, then to Italy, living there until 1822. In 1823
set out for Greece, to help in war of independence
against Turks, and died of fever at Missolonghi.

Byron: The Poems, edited by G. Pocock, revised by V. de
Sola Pinto, 1963.

10 Victorians, 1837 - 1901

**Alfred, Lord
Tennyson
1809–92**

Born in Lincolnshire. Educated at Cambridge, where he
became a member of an intellectual group, the
'Apostles', of which Arthur Hallam was a member.
Published his first individual book, 1830. The death of
Hallam in 1833 began the process of composing 'In
Memoriam' (not published until 1850). Meanwhile, his
two-volume *Poems* (1842) and *The Princess* (1847)
established his reputation, which by 1850 was so high
that he was appointed Poet Laureate on Wordsworth's
death. That same year he married, and lived thereafter
on the Isle of Wight and in Surrey. The chief volumes
of poems of these later years are *Maud* (1855), *The Idylls
of the King* (begun in the early 1840s, but not published
in full until 1889), and *Tiresias and Other Poems* (1885).

Tennyson: The Poems, edited by Christopher Ricks, 1969.

**Emily Brontë
1818–48**

Born in Yorkshire, sister of Anne and Charlotte. Lived
in Haworth from the age of two until her death.
Educated in Yorkshire and Brussels. Taught in Halifax
briefly. Published *Poems* with her two sisters,
pseudonymously, in 1846, and *Wuthering Heights*, also
pseudonymously, in 1847.

Emily Brontë: Poems, edited by Rosemary Hartill, 1973.

**Dante Gabriel
Rossetti
1828–82**

Born in London. Educated at King's College, London,
and then studied drawing and painting.
Founder–member of the Pre-Raphaelite Brotherhood of
artists and writers, 1848. From then on, mainly a
painter, but also a copious poet and translator. For the
last dozen or so years of his life, suffered from physical

and mental troubles, partly caused by his drug addiction.

Poems, edited by Oswald Doughty, 1957.

Christina Rossetti 1830–94
Born in London, sister of Dante Gabriel. Educated privately, and began to contribute to the Pre-Raphaelite magazine, *The Germ*, in 1850. Her first great success was the publication of *Goblin Market and Other Poems* in 1862. She lived a secluded life, looking after her mother and giving herself to church work and devotional writing. She was an invalid for many years until her death.

The Poetical Works, edited by William Rossetti, 1904.

Robert Browning 1812–89
Born in London. Mainly educated at home, and supported by his father until he married Elizabeth Barrett at the age of thirty-four. He wrote prolifically from an early age, but only began to have any real success in the early 1840s. Even then, it was not until *Men and Women* (1855) that he achieved anything like the reputation of his wife as a poet. Lived in Italy with her, 1846–61, and after her death largely lived in London. From about 1870 he was seen as the only possible rival to Tennyson: by the time he died, there were many branches of the Browning Society.

Robert Browning: The Poems, edited by J. Pettigrew and T. J. Collins, 1981.

Matthew Arnold 1822–88
Born in Middlesex, the son of Dr Thomas Arnold, later Headmaster of Rugby; educated at Rugby and Oxford. For most of his life, from 1851 until he retired in 1883, he was an Inspector of Schools. Most of his best poems were written between 1849 and 1855. Later, he concentrated on prose, with a large number of political, social, theological and literary critical books, most importantly *Culture and Anarchy* (1869).

Matthew Arnold: Poems, edited by Kenneth Allott, 1965.

Algernon Charles Swinburne 1837–1909
Born in London. Educated at Oxford, but left without a degree. Lived in London, becoming well-known with *Poems and Ballads* (1866), and associating with the Pre-Raphaelite circle. Taken into care in Putney in 1879 by Theodore Watts-Dunton, with whom he lived for the rest of his life.

Works of Algernon Charles Swinburne, edited by Edmund
Gosse and T. J. Wise, 1925–7.

11   American Pioneers, 1849-1910

Edgar Allan Poe
1809–49

Born in Boston. Orphaned when an infant and taken
into the household of a Virginia merchant. Educated at
school in England (1816–20), Virginia, and at the
University of Virginia for a short time. Briefly served in
the US Army. Mainly worked as a journalist, in Virginia,
Pennsylvania and New York. Published four books of
poems and four books of fiction (including *Tales of the
Grotesque and Arabesque*, 1840) between 1827 and his
death.

The Complete Poems of Edgar Allan Poe, edited by Richard
Wilbur, 1959.

Walt Whitman
1819–92

Born in New York. Left school at eleven and
successively worked as an office boy, printer's
apprentice, newspaper writer (and sometimes editor),
carpenter, nurse and minor civil servant. *Leaves of Grass*,
first published at his own expense in 1855, went into
several revised editions throughout his life, and was
followed by seven other books of poems, as well as such
prose works as *Democratic Vistas* (1870). During the last
eight years of his life he lived in Camden, New Jersey,
where he was visited by many admirers.

Walt Whitman: The Complete Poems, edited by Francis
Murphy, 1975.

Julia Ward Howe
1819–1910

Born in New York (*née* Ward). With her husband she
edited an anti-slavery paper in Boston. Wrote
biographies and social criticism, and was a pioneer of
the women's suffrage movement. Her books of poems
include *Passion Flowers* (1854) and *Later Lyrics* (1866).

Herman Melville
1819–91

Born in New York. In his teens, became a sailor on
merchant and sailing ships. Deserted ship in the Pacific
in 1842 and returned to America via Tahiti. Wrote
about such adventures in his early romances. *Moby Dick*
published 1850. Its unpopularity, and the general

unpopularity of his later books, made him write poetry, which he published privately.

Collected Poems of Herman Melville, edited by H. P. Vincent, 1947.

Emily Dickinson 1830–86

Born in Massachusetts, and hardly left the family house in Amherst throughout her life. Her first poems date from about 1850, but most were written between 1859 and her death, with the early and mid 1860s being particularly prolific. Sent a few poems to Thomas Higginson, an essayist and lecturer, in 1862; impressed but puzzled, he tried to advise her and was responsible for publishing some of her poems in periodicals. But she died four years before the publication of her first small volume.

The Complete Poems of Emily Dickinson, edited by Thomas H. Johnson, 1970.

Edwin Arlington Robinson 1869–1935

Born and brought up in Maine. Went to Harvard, but left after two years when his family ran out of money. Started as a freelance writer, without success. Settled in New York in the late 1890s and held various minor jobs, including subway construction inspector. His poetry was read and praised by President Theodore Roosevelt, who gave him a job in the United States Customs in New York. His book of poems, *The Man Against the Sky* (1916), made enough money for him to live on, and his work continued to sell. But he lived an isolated life, and was preoccupied with failure and regret.

Collected Poems, 1937.

12 Romantics and Realists, 1870 - 1920

Thomas Hardy 1840–1928

Born in Dorset. Educated at local schools and at home, until he was articled to a Dorchester architect in 1856. Settled in London in 1861, to practise architecture, but gave it up in the late 1860s to write. Published his first novel in 1871, and thereafter published seventeen more until *Jude the Obscure* appeared in 1896. *Wessex Poems* was published in 1898, and he continued to write and

publish poems until the end of his life. Lived at Max
Gate, Dorchester, from 1886. Married twice: to Emma
Gifford (who died in 1912), and in 1914 to Florence
Dugdale, who survived him.

Complete Poems of Thomas Hardy, edited by James
Gibson, 1976.

**Gerard Manley
Hopkins
1844–89**

Born in London. Educated there and at Oxford, where
he became a Roman Catholic convert, entering the Jesuit
Novitiate in 1868 and being ordained priest in 1877. He
served as a priest in London, Oxford, Liverpool and
Glasgow between 1877 and 1882, when he went to
teach classics at Stonyhurst, the Catholic school, for two
years. He was Professor of Greek at University College,
Dublin, from 1884 until his death. He showed his
poems to three friends, Robert Bridges, R. W. Dixon
and Coventry Patmore, all of them poets; but Bridges
decided not to publish him until a collection finally
appeared in 1918.

The Poems of Gerard Manley Hopkins, edited by
W. H. Gardner, 1956.

**A. E. Housman
1859–1936**

Born in Worcestershire, and educated there and at
Oxford, where – though a brilliant scholar – he failed
his final examinations. For ten years he worked as a
clerk in the Patent Office in London, following his own
course of classical studies, until in 1892 he was
appointed Professor of Latin at University College,
London, and then Professor of Latin at Cambridge in
1911. He published *A Shropshire Lad*, at first at his own
expense, in 1896.

The Collected Poems of A. E. Housman, edited by
J. W. Carter, 1939.

**Rudyard Kipling
1865–1936**

Born in Bombay, went to school in Devon, and on his
return to India worked as a journalist in Lahore,
1882–9. Then settled in London and became a full-time
writer, having already published several books of prose
and verse. He was a prolific writer of fiction, poetry,
children's books, travel books and much else. He was
awarded the Nobel Prize for Literature in 1907.

Verse (definitive edition), 1940.

13 Early Twentieth Century, 1914-39

W. B. Yeats
1865–1939

Born in Dublin, son of Anglo-Irish parents (his father was a painter), and brought up partly in London. Studied art in Dublin in the mid 1880s, and published his first full-length book of poems in 1886. He lived mainly in London, 1890–1921, but was closely involved in Irish nationalist politics, and with the Irish theatre, helping to found the Abbey Theatre in Dublin in 1904. He settled in Ireland in 1922, though he continued to travel a great deal. He served in the Irish Senate, 1922–8, and was awarded the Nobel Prize for Literature in 1923. Though a well-known poet by the turn of the century, it was with his book *Responsibilities* (1914) that he began to emerge as a major figure.

Collected Poems of W. B. Yeats, 1950.

Wilfred Owen
1893–1918

Born in Shropshire, brought up there and in Cheshire. Worked as a tutor in English in France, 1913–14. Joined the army in 1915, went to France in 1916, and was invalided home the following year. In August 1918 he returned to the front, and was killed in action one week before the Armistice. The first collection of his poems, edited by Siegfried Sassoon, whom he had met in a military hospital in 1917, was published posthumously in 1920.

Collected Poems of Wilfred Owen, edited by C. Day-Lewis, 1963

Edward Thomas
1878–1917

Born in London, educated there and at Oxford, where he married while still a student. For most of his life worked as a journalist, reviewer and freelance writer, earning a precarious living. Met Robert Frost in 1913 and with his encouragement soon began writing verse, little of which was published before he was killed in action in France in 1917.

Collected Poems of Edward Thomas, edited by R. George Thomas, 1978.

Robert Frost
1874–1963

Born in California, but moved soon to New England, going to Harvard but leaving without a degree. Worked as a teacher and farmer. Lived in England, 1912–15. Soon after his return to America, having started to make his reputation as a poet, he began a series of appointments as writer-in-residence at various universities.

Robert Frost: The Poetry, edited by Edward Connery Latham, 1969.

T. S. Eliot
1888–1965

Born in St Louis, Missouri, and educated there and at Harvard. Studied in Munich, Paris and Oxford, 1910–15. Worked as a teacher, then as a bank clerk, in England, 1915–25. Joined the staff of the publishers, Faber and Gwyer (later Faber and Faber) in 1926, becoming a director and working there until his death. Edited the *Criterion* magazine, 1922–39. Took British nationality in 1927, and the same year was confirmed as a member of the Church of England. His first book (*Prufrock and Other Observations*) was published in 1917, and after that his most important verse is *The Waste Land* (1922) and *Four Quartets* (each Quartet published separately between 1935 and 1942, and then together in 1943). He also wrote six plays, beginning with *The Rock* and *Murder in the Cathedral* in 1934 and 1935, and ending with *The Elder Statesman* in 1958. He was awarded the Nobel Prize for Literature in 1948. He also published much literary criticism.

The Complete Poems and Plays of T. S. Eliot, 1969.

W. H. Auden
1907–73

Born in York. Educated in Norfolk and at Oxford. Worked as a schoolmaster, 1930–35, and in the later 1930s travelled a great deal, throughout Europe and in China. In 1939 went to the United States, settling there and becoming an American citizen in 1946. He taught at various American universities, but returned to England and to his old college at Oxford shortly before his death. He was a well-known and influential poet from the publication of his first book, *Poems*, in 1930, and went on to become the dominant poet of the 1930s. He continued to be a prolific writer of poems, plays, opera libretti, literary essays and much else.

Collected Poems of W. H. Auden, edited by Edward Mendelson, 1976.

Louis MacNeice   Born in Belfast, educated at Marlborough and Oxford.
1907–63   He was a university lecturer in classics until 1941, when
he joined the BBC as a radio writer and producer.
There he remained, apart from some short periods
lecturing abroad, until his sudden death from pneumonia.

Collected Poems, edited by E. R. Dodds, 1966.

John Betjeman   Born in London, educated there, at Marlborough and at
1906–84   Oxford. He was for a time a schoolmaster, then a
journalist, but soon established himself as a broadcaster
and writer on architecture and topography, as well as a
poet. He was knighted in 1969 and was appointed Poet
Laureate in 1972.

Collected Poems, 1972 (revised edition).

14 Later Twentieth Century, 1934-84

Dylan Thomas   Born and educated in Swansea. Worked briefly as a
1914–53   journalist on a local newspaper, but from 1933 onwards
was a freelance writer and, later, radio broadcaster. His
first book, *Eighteen Poems*, was published in 1934, and he
published four other books of poems, including a
Collected Poems, in his lifetime. He also wrote his radio
'play for voices', *Under Milk Wood*, and many stories and
radio pieces. He was invited to the United States to give
poetry readings in 1950, 1952 and 1953, and died (of
'insult to the brain') during the last of these, in New
York.

The Poems, edited by Daniel Jones, 1971.

Robert Lowell   Born in Boston, educated at Harvard and at Kenyon
1917–77   College, Ohio. Registered as a conscientious objector
during the Second World War, and was for a time in
prison. From 1949 chiefly employed as a university
teacher. Married three times. Published his first book,
Land of Unlikeness, in 1944, and his first major book,
Lord Weary's Castle, in 1946. He was a prolific writer,
constantly revising, and there is as yet no full-scale
Collected Poems.

Selected Poems, 1976

Philip Larkin
1922–

Born in Coventry, educated there and at Oxford. Since 1943 he has been a librarian, and since 1955 has been Librarian of the University of Hull. He published a book of poems and two novels in the 1940s, but his three important books are *The Less Deceived* (1955), *The Whitsun Weddings* (1964) and *High Windows* (1974). He also edited *The Oxford Book of Twentieth Century English Verse* (1973), and has published a collection of prose pieces, *Required Writing* (1983).

Robert Graves
1895–

Born in London, educated at Charterhouse. Served in the army during the First World War, and afterwards went up to Oxford. Apart from a year as Professor of English at Cairo University in the 1920s, he has earned his living as a copious writer, of novels, translations, books on mythology, biographies and much else, as well as poetry. Lived on Majorca during the early 1930s, and returned there after the Second World War.

Collected Poems, 1975.

Ted Hughes
1930–

Born in the West Riding of Yorkshire, educated there and at Cambridge. In 1956 he married Sylvia Plath. For most of his life he has been a freelance writer, and has published over ten books of poems, as well as many plays, children's books and miscellaneous writing.

Selected Poems 1957–1981, 1982.

Sylvia Plath
1932–63

Born in Boston, Massachusetts, educated at Smith College and at Cambridge. She married Ted Hughes in 1956, had two children, and after separation from her husband committed suicide in London in 1963. She published only two books in her lifetime: a volume of poems (*The Colossus*, 1960) and a novel (*The Bell Jar*, 1963).

Collected Poems, edited by Ted Hughes, 1981.

Acknowledgements

We wish to thank the following for permission to reprint their copyright material:

Curtis Brown Ltd for 'Musée des Beaux Arts' and for Sonnet VIII from *In Time of War* by W. H. Auden, copyright the Estate of W. H. Auden.

Jonathan Cape Ltd and the Estate of Robert Frost for 'Stopping by Woods on a Snowy Evening' and 'Mending Wall' by Robert Frost from *The Poetry of Robert Frost*, edited by Edward Connery Lathem.

J. M. Dent & Sons Ltd for 'The Force that through the Green Fuse Drives the Flower' and 'Do Not Go Gentle into That Good Night' by Dylan Thomas from *Collected Poems*.

Faber & Faber Ltd for 'A Game of Chess' from *The Waste Land – Part 2* by T. S. Eliot, from *Collected Poems 1909–1962*; for 'The Thought-Fox' from *Hawk in the Rain* by Ted Hughes; for 'The Explosion' from *High Windows* by Philip Larkin; for 'Skunk Hour' from *Life Studies* and 'For the Union Dead' by Robert Lowell and for 'Soap Suds' by Louis MacNeice from *Collected Poems*.

Robert Graves for 'The Cool Web'.

Olwyn Hughes for 'Among the Narcissi' by Sylvia Plath. © Ted Hughes 1971.

The Marvell Press, England for 'Church Going' by Philip Larkin, from *The Less Deceived*.

John Murray for 'NW5 & N6' by John Betjeman, from *John Betjeman's Collected Poems*. Copyright © John Betjeman.

The National Trust for 'The Story of Uriah' by Rudyard Kipling and the National Trust and Methuen London Ltd for 'Danny Deever' by Rudyard Kipling.

The Society of Authors as the literary representative of the Estate of A. E. Housman, and Jonathan Cape Ltd as publishers for 'Tell Me not here' and 'In valleys green and still' by A. E. Housman from *Collected Poems*.

Michael Yeats and Macmillan London Ltd for 'An Irish Airman Foresees his Death', 'The Second Coming', 'Leda and the Swan' and 'Politics' by W. B. Yeats.

Part of *The Prologue* and *The Pardoner's Tale* by Geoffrey Chaucer are from Chaucer, *The Canterbury Tales*, translated by Nevill Coghill (Penguin Classics, Revised edition 1977), pages 19–20, 37–8, 268–74. Copyright 1951. Nevill Coghill. Copyright © Nevill Coghill, 1958, 1960, 1975, 1977. Reprinted by permission of Penguin Books Ltd.

'Miniver Cheevy' by Edwin Arlington Robinson is reprinted with the permission of Charles Scribner's Sons from *The Town Down the River*. Copyright 1910 Charles Scribner's Sons; copyright renewed 1938 Ruth Nivison.

Index

Page numbers in bold refer to biographical entries.